I0763151

A Confessor's Companion

A Confessor's Companion

TENDER CONSCIENCE *and* SCRUPULOSITY

Rev. Thomas M. Santa, CSsR

Catholic. Pastoral. Trusted.

Helping the Scrupulous Penitent Find Peace

Some people of God are unable to believe that God loves and accepts them. No word calms their aching spirits, and assurances of God's grace have seemingly little or no effect. The manifestations of scrupulosity are most often experienced by penitents during the sacrament of reconciliation.

The good news is that you needn't be a professional therapist or even well-schooled in personality disorders to help penitents with OCD-based scrupulosity. You just need to be able to recognize the disorder when it is manifested and be willing to take the next steps.

This handbook for confessors provides the pastoral applications that are necessary to help the penitent truly celebrate the sacrament of reconciliation. And instead of a chamber of torture, the confessional will be a place to experience the outpouring of God's grace and mercy.

Imprimi Potest:
Kevin Zubel, CSsR, Provincial
Denver Province, The Redemptorists

Published by Liguori Publications
Liguori, Missouri 63057

Liguori Publications, a nonprofit corporation,
is an apostolate of the Redemptorists (Redemptorists.com).
To order, visit Liguori.org or call 800-325-9521

ISBN 978-0-7648- 2911-6
E-ISBN 978-0-7648-7291-4

Library of Congress Cataloging-in-Publication Data
Names: Santa, Thomas M., 1952- author
Title: A confessor's companion : tender conscience and scrupulosity / Rev. Thomas M. Santa, CSsR.

Description: First edition | Liguori, Missouri : Liguori Publications, [2026] | Includes bibliographical references. | Summary: "Rev. Thomas M. Santa draws from his many years of ministry to the scrupulous and advises priest confessors about helping penitents who have a tender conscience or OCD-based scrupulosity"-- Provided by publisher.
Identifiers: LCCN 2026014123 (print) | LCCN 2026014124 (ebook) | ISBN 9780764829116 paperback | ISBN 9780764872914 ebook
Subjects: LCSH: Scruples | Confession--Catholic Church | Pastoral counseling
Classification: LCC BJ1278.S37 S256 2026 (print) | LCC BJ1278.S37 (ebook)
LC record available at https://lccn.loc.gov/2026014123
LC ebook record available at https://lccn.loc.gov/2026014124

Printed in the United States of America
30 29 28 27 26 / 5 4 3 2 1
First edition

Contents

Preface

I hope this book will be a pastoral help for those who accompany a scrupulous person on his or her healing journey. Although it is primarily intended for the priest confessor, this book is also appropriate for any therapist, spiritual director, mentor, friend, or family member who is willing to walk with a scrupulous person on the journey toward healing.

This book is the result of thousands of individual spiritual-direction sessions with men and women who suffer with the scrupulous disorder. I have engaged in the ministry of spiritual direction for the scrupulous for more than thirty years, during which I have written a monthly newsletter, *Scrupulous Anonymous*. I have answered daily the urgent questions of people who contact me. I have conducted numerous retreats and days of recollection, and I have filmed more than fifty videos on a variety of subjects that speak to the scrupulous condition. I have engaged in individual counseling, averaging two consultations a day and group work on the weekends. It has been a real privilege to work with the scrupulous, but it has not even begun to reach the core group of people who suffer with this disorder. People with scrupulosity are often alone and ignored, in the shadows of day-to-day living, quietly and desperately hoping for some kind of relief that never seems to come.

I believe the most effective path to ministry for scrupulous people is one that is both local and personal—face to face when possible. If the local parish priest, spiritual director, or therapist can gain an understanding of and sensitivity to the scrupulous condition, then miracles can happen. Real healing is possible, but it will take quite a bit of intensely focused pastoral care, not to mention an abundance of God's grace.

It is painful to try to understand, perhaps for the first time, the ravages of scrupulosity. It is challenging, particularly for priest confessors, to accept and that what they think they know about the disorder is often inadequate. It will be hard to resist the urge to comfort and reassure and instead to choose the necessary pastoral remedy that will enable the scrupulous person to experience the grace of God. At times, the pastoral remedy may seem insufficient; at other times, it may seem to lack empathy. It is not. Scrupulosity is very serious, and it requires a very disciplined application of pastoral care.

The confessor, therapist, spiritual director, or friend must carefully choose how best to apply the pastoral care outlined in these pages. Not everything is appropriate for every scrupulous person. Carefully listening to and discerning the truth(s) that are shared with you—often from the most vulnerable and intimate actions, events, and even memories—will help you guide the scrupulous person to where they need to be for healing. I firmly believe that your best efforts are completely dependent on the grace of God, and all you are doing is enabling a path for that grace to become animated.

When I first started working with the scrupulous more than thirty years ago, I never thought it would become a lifelong ministry. I never thought I was to be more than a placeholder in the long line of Redemptorist directors of Scrupulous Anonymous. That, however, seems not to have been God's plan, and I must admit that I am grateful.

Through this ministry, I have encountered some of the most compassionate and loving people. Men and women who are generous, kind, discerning, prayerful, and deeply spiritual but also who do not believe, even for a minute, that they are good and loving. Scrupulosity is a voice that always condemns. That always tells them what is wrong or incomplete in their lives. That is never satisfied with any of their efforts. That always promises clarity and certainty as the reward for engaging in the obsessions and compulsions it demands. But it is a lie. Nothing that scrupulosity proposes is in the least bit truthful. It is a cruel lie.

Unfortunately, if you are a Catholic who struggles with scrupulosity, your suffering is perhaps even more intense. Catholic moral teaching covers every possible question. This is the result of hundreds of years of meditation, scholarly thinking, and lived experience, all of which is beneficial for the person who needs help to understand sin and how it affects his or her life. For the scrupulous person, however, it is not a help; it is a system that torments them at every turn. Every exception, every nuance, every discernible application—often effortlessly used by people without scrupulosity—is just one more rigid rule and regulation. One more obstacle, one more overwhelming challenge, one more burden. If you are scrupulous, you know this all too well as the truth and as your day-to-day experience of life.

Rev. Thomas M. Santa, CSsR

"They repent when they
have not sinned,
and accuse themselves
without form or matter;
their virtues make them tremble
and in their innocence
they are afraid."

— Jeremy Taylor
(cited in *Three Hundred Years of Psychiatry*, 1535-1860)

Introduction

On many occasions, Pope Francis of blessed memory stated that priests are called to be "ministers of mercy." He referenced this calling in discussions on the priest's role in the sacrament of reconciliation. He gently reminded priests that the mercy of Jesus is a primary focus in all aspects of their vocation. As a priest and confessor, I understand that my brother priests appreciate the former Pope's perspective. We strive to pastorally apply mercy, understanding, and reconciliation in and out of the confessional.

Most people of God appreciate the efforts of their priests and perceive the sacrament of reconciliation as a reminder of God's love, which is a life-giving and grace-filled love. Yet, despite their priest/pastor/confessor's best ministerial efforts, some people of God are unable to believe that God loves and accepts them. No word calms their aching spirits, and assurances of God's grace have seemingly little or no effect.

Their inability to accept and believe in God's saving mercy isn't the result of stubbornness or hardness of heart. Rather, it is usually the manifestation of *scrupulosity,* a disorder that floods the mind and heart with "a thousand frightening fantasies," as Dr. Joseph W. Ciarrocchi so powerfully described in his book *The Doubting Disease.*

The manifestations of scrupulosity are most often experienced by priest and penitent during the sacrament of reconciliation. The penitent's disconnected, pain-filled voice fills the darkness of the confessional. What's intended to be a sacramental celebration is instead something much less than what the penitent hoped for or imagined. Instead, priest and penitent witness the penitent's recitation of perceived sin after perceived sin, frequently punctuated with expressions of doubt and numerous questions. It is tortuous for both priest and penitent.

I deliberately describe the experience as "disconnected" because the priest struggles to connect with the penitent, and the penitent is struggling to connect with the priest as a "minister of mercy." The penitent performs a complex ritual that expresses a sustained struggle marked by anxiety, guilt, and profound loneliness. The expressionless confession of a litany of sins—most of which are only *perceived* failures of commission or omission, rooted in the fear of sin—is the final step in the ritual.

Unfortunately, when the confession has concluded and the ritual completed, the penitent experiences no assurance of mercy, no experience of inner calm and peace, and no conviction of reconciliation or God's mercy. Instead, a new obsessive or compulsive ritual begins. Moreover, the priest also experiences a different type of frustration and is often perplexed about how he might respond with understanding and compassion.

Although people with scrupulosity enter the confessional hoping to experience relief from their torment, they also understand that mechanical recitation of perceived sin is useless. This is where the disconnect occurs: They want to no longer be in this situation, but they're caught up in the ritual. Both priest and penitent witness the power of an experience each would prefer to avoid.

What I'm describing isn't the traditional "tender conscience" type of scrupulosity routinely discussed in seminary classes on the ministry of reconciliation. A tender conscience, although painful, isn't permanent. Patience and good catechetical training will eventually win out; anxiety and doubt will be significantly reduced; and the penitent will be able to enjoy and truly celebrate the sacrament of reconciliation.

The type of scrupulosity I am referring to is a manifestation of obsessive-compulsive disorder (OCD). Priests must be able to recognize the difference between a person with a tender conscience and a person with OCD-based scrupulosity. Priests must understand that OCD is a behavioral and emotional disorder with many specific manifestations, only one of which is religious scrupulosity. This is not a matter of opinion. It is not a statement of so-called "wokeness" or an indication of "modernism." What I am describing is mental illness, not spiritual weakness.

The good news is that you needn't be a professional therapist or even well schooled in personality disorders to help penitents with OCD-based scrupulosity. You just need to be able to recognize the disorder when it is manifested and be willing to take the next steps.

There is essentially no difference in the psychological and emotional roots of OCD from one person to the next. What differs is the manifestation. Many people with OCD focus on a fear of germs or forgetting to lock the door, turn off the oven, or perform some other routine task. People with OCD often have more than one manifestation, although one concern tends to dominate. In OCD scrupulosity, the questions and doubts focus on sin. Even though the penitent is using the language of sin, they are not describing sinful choices or behaviors. They describe anxiety, guilt, and shame and use the language of sin to explain what they are experiencing. Unfortunately, they often do not understand the difference; they believe they are talking about sin and their relationship with God. As a confessor, you need to know the difference and understand the reality.

OCD tries the patience of both priests and penitents, especially if the wrong pastoral remedy is applied. Empathy, not catechetics, is required. If OCD scrupulosity could be managed with catechesis, the penitent could have been healed long ago. Men and women with OCD scrupulosity are some of the best-catechized people in the world! They are totally dedicated to researching their faith and do not hesitate to crack open the *Catechism of the Catholic Church* or the *Code of Canon Law* to quell their persistent doubts and clarify their questions. Sadly, they painfully discover that knowledge and content satisfy nothing. More information produces more questions, fueling the disorder instead of healing it.

So, what should you do? What is the most helpful pastoral response? That is the purpose of this book. My hope is that it will benefit you as a confessor in making the pastoral applications necessary to help penitents with OCD scrupulosity truly celebrate the sacrament of reconciliation.

Please note that in the pages that follow, I refrain from repeatedly referencing "OCD scrupulosity." For the sake of clarity, and because this is intended as a pastoral companion and not a psychological journal, I simply designate the disorder as "scrupulosity." Please also note that this pastoral companion does not replace the traditional and very wise direction of the saints through the centuries who have helped us understand the tender conscience. The material presented here is not meant to be applied to those with a tender conscience; it is for those men and women who are tormented by OCD scrupulosity.

In a 2013 homily, Pope Francis reminded the people of God that the confessional is not intended to be a torture chamber. If a priest is aware of the ravages of OCD and is willing to apply the correct pastoral advice and direction, he can substantially reduce the pain and suffering of scrupulosity. And instead of a chamber of torture, the confessional will become a place for the scrupulous to experience the outpouring of God's grace and mercy.

NOTES

CHAPTER ONE

The Traditional Understanding of Scrupulosity

When I talk to priests, it isn't uncommon for the subject of scrupulosity to come up, because many of them know that I minister to people who suffer with the scrupulous condition. Often, the first reaction is an "eye roll" and an expression of sympathy: "I really do not know how you do this day in and day out."

This response is not disrespectful, but it is revealing. The revelation effectively summarizes at least two perceptions: first, the familiarity that the priest confessor has with scrupulous people; second, the frustration the priest confessor often experiences in the encounter.

Although all priest confessors have some kind of experience with scrupulosity, most have no real understanding about what they are encountering, so they default to what they know. However, what they know can be woefully inadequate. Their seminary training, for the most part, introduced them to the concept of a "tender conscience." The traditional pastoral care for a person with a tender conscience is for the person to place all of his or her trust in the direction of the confessor and resist the urge to ask for reassurance from other confessors. This is sound advice if this is truly a person with a tender conscience, but it is incomplete advice if there is something else—such as the scrupulous disorder—going on.

The traditional understanding of scrupulosity as a manifestation of a tender conscience refers to a conscience that is highly sensitive to right and wrong and often inclined toward deep moral seriousness, humility, and a strong desire to avoid sin. It is not necessarily problematic from a psychological perspective, but it can develop into a problem if not formed well or guided well.

A tender conscience is:

- easily moved by moral or spiritual concerns.
- quick to feel guilt or remorse when the person believes he or she has done wrong.
- deeply attuned to the will of God and the demands of love and justice.
- often found in holy people, saints, and sincere Christians who fear offending God.

"The fear of the Lord is the beginning of wisdom" (Psalm 111:10). A tender conscience often springs from holy reverence, not irrational fear.

What makes a tender conscience confusing to both the penitent and the confessor is the perspective offered by the saints who said that a well-formed and spiritually mature tender conscience can:

- lead to greater compassion and moral integrity.
- foster repentance and humility.
- guard against rationalization or complacency.
- inspire deeper prayer and dependence on grace.

However, this is where pastoral sensitivity is required, because there are potential dangers associated with a tender conscience. If not properly formed or if distorted by anxiety, a tender conscience can:

- trigger OCD scrupulosity.
- lead to excessive self-blame or fear of damnation.
- undermine trust in God's mercy.
- become overly focused on perfection, minor faults, or imagined sins.

Tender Versus Scrupulous Conscience

Aspect	**Tender Conscience**	**Scrupulous Conscience**
Sensitivity	High, but balanced by trust and love	Extreme, often dominated by fear
Focus	On love, repentance, and growth	On guilt, punishment, and self-doubt
Moral Judgment	Accurate and formed by truth	Inaccurate, often confused or rigid
Spiritual Fruit	Peace, humility, closeness to God	Anxiety, despair, spiritual paralysis

It will come as no surprise to the priest confessor that the person who exhibits a tender conscience will be well versed in their condition. People with scrupulosity and those with a tender conscience spend hours doing research about their condition. By the time they encounter the priest in the confessional, they aren't necessarily there to play out their scrupulous ritual; rather, they're seeking pastoral counseling and guidance—and they will have done their homework beforehand! For example, they may have researched the Church's saints who struggled with a tender conscience:

St. Alphonsus Liguori (1696–1787)

- Patron of the scrupulous and moral theologians.
- Struggled with scrupulosity in his early life but developed a theology centered on God's mercy and the gentle guidance of conscience.
- Advised the scrupulous to "go against" their fears when not grounded in clear reason or Church teaching.

"A single act of perfect love is enough to make a soul holy."

St. Thérèse of Lisieux (1873–1897)

- Known for her "Little Way" of trust and love.
- As a child, she was deeply conscientious and felt distress over small faults but matured into a saint who surrendered everything to divine mercy.
- Her spirituality liberated her conscience from anxiety and centered it on God's love, not perfectionism.

"What pleases him is to see me love my littleness and poverty."

St. Ignatius of Loyola (1491–1556)

- Early in his conversion, he became overly scrupulous and despairing of salvation.
- Through discernment, he learned to distinguish between true movements of the Spirit and those rooted in anxiety or deception.
- His *Spiritual Exercises* help the faithful properly form and guide their consciences.

"It is not hard to find God, if only one desires to find Him."

St. Catherine of Siena (1347–1380)

- From a young age, she had a profound desire not to offend God in even the smallest ways.
- Her tender conscience was balanced by an extraordinary boldness in loving God and serving the Church, even confronting popes when necessary.

"Be who God meant you to be, and you will set the world on fire."

St. John Vianney (1786–1859)

- Possessed a deep sensitivity to sin and spent long hours in the confessional, guiding others gently.
- Though he sometimes doubted his worthiness, he placed his trust entirely in God's grace and mercy.

"The saints did not all begin well, but they ended well."

For the purposes of this pastoral companion, the basic information provided is more than sufficient for the effective pastoral direction of the priest confessor and his relationship with the penitent who manifests a tender conscience. If, upon reflection, it is the discerning and informed opinion of the priest confessor that there is no psychological component (i.e., obsession, compulsion, panic, anxiety, etc.), he can be assured that the traditional pastoral remedy for the person with a tender conscience can be applied.

However, if the discernment indicates the presence of a psychological disorder, it is irresponsible to apply the traditional remedy. It is irresponsible because the confessor is effectively enabling the disorder and prolonging the suffering of the penitent. He may believe otherwise and even have a strong conviction that he is doing all that is required, but that does not change the reality. Something more is required.

As people of faith, we of course believe in the power of prayer, the ordinary manifestation of God's grace and love, and the possibility of miracles. Acknowledging the presence of a disorder does not contradict what we believe. At the same time, we have a responsibility to use the gifts that the Lord has given us in service to the people of God. I believe the implementation of a pastoral remedy that goes beyond the Tradition is sometimes necessary. It does not have to be the first choice, but it does need to be one of the options if we are to serve the people of God responsibly.

CHAPTER TWO

When Scrupulosity Is More than a Tender Conscience

If you recognize the presence of a possible psychological disorder, the first step in directing penitents toward a way of healthy spiritual living is not complicated. Instead of instructing or catechizing them, which is appropriate for the tender conscience but not for OCD scrupulosity, choose to engage them in a conversation. Let them know that you feel and understand their pain and suffering. It's often difficult for penitents to hear their confessor share this insight, but, eventually, after months of confessions, they may accept your offer of spiritual guidance and support by *asking for* help and direction. Only then can you effectively respond with focused pastoral care. This requires a great deal of time and commitment from both priest and penitent. It will be difficult, but it is worth the effort.

While you are waiting for the penitent to realize that he or she needs something more, please be patient and, above all, do not make matters worse. When you recognize the obsessive and compulsive ritual of a scrupulous confession, resist the urge to try and "fix" it. You cannot. Resist the urge to reassure the person that everything is OK. It is not. Do not do anything but listen, remind the penitent that you are willing to help, and then provide penance and offer the prayer of absolution. You may feel like this is an inadequate response, but it is the best and most loving response of all. You are not enabling the disorder; you are helping the person take a necessary step on the path to healing.

After some time, which may include a false start or two along the way, you can engage the necessary pastoral response and care. When you and the penitent have determined together that the next step is to take the conversation out of the confessional and bring it to a more suitable venue for talking, schedule an appointment for the two of you. In the context of focused spiritual direction, inform the penitent that you are only one of several required resources that will help him or her. Gently inform the person that what he or she is struggling with is a mental disorder that generates strong religious imagery, which intensifies the suffering. This person is not responsible in any manner for these images or thoughts; the scrupulous disorder is generating them to produce anxiety.

It will be helpful to the penitent if you compassionately share what is happening in his or her mind because of the disorder. You are not sharing this to provide the person with something he or she doesn't already know; rather, this is one way for you to help the person appreciate that you do, in fact, understand what he or she is experiencing.

For people with the scrupulosity disorder, the obsessive and compulsive response to whatever "triggers" him or her begins with some sort of event or experience that is then summarized by an impulsive thought that is generated. I would like to note here that although I use the term "impulsive thought" to refer to this response to the OCD trigger, I think that "phantom thought," a classification often used by practitioners of inference-based cognitive behavioral therapy (I-CBT), might be more helpful. As of this writing, though, I have not developed the necessary narrative to completely support a change in emphasis, so I retain the traditional designation of "impulsive thought."

This is how the scrupulous person responds to the impulsive thought:

1. I did it.
2. I know I did it.
3. I know it is my choice.
4. It is offensive to God.

5. I must stop it, fix it, or control it.
6. If I do not stop it, fix it, or control it, I am going to hell.

Scrupulous people can be very literal at times, so it may be necessary to adjust the key word of the obsessive litany: instead of "I did it," it might be "I thought it," "I said it," "I ate it," or any of a multitude of possible meanings. What the confessor needs to understand is that the path from number 1 to number 6 is ***instantaneous***.

For people without scrupulosity, given the same circumstances, their response to the impulsive thought is this: nothing. They pay it no heed, at most asking themselves, *I wonder where that came from?* See the difference? Both responses are real, not imagined, but one response is spiritually and mentally exhausting, while the other response is basically harmless. The former is what you encounter with a scrupulous person.

When you share with the scrupulous penitent that you understand what he or she is experiencing, you help the person appreciate this conversation as a moment of God's grace in his or her life. Grace has made it possible for this sacred moment to happen. Grace has made it possible for the penitent to start recognizing that it is not enough to bring these concerns to the confessional and that he or she requires psychological therapy, supported by spiritual direction. The core message of this conversation is that you will work with the penitent to seek good psychological health and well-being to complement and support your spiritual care.

Expect resistance, even if the penitent understands that this is the best way to manage the disorder. Many people with scrupulosity mistrust psychologists, behavior-modification techniques, and even prescription drug therapy. Some have a deeply held perception that scrupulosity is their personal cross and that by learning to manage the disorder, they are displeasing the Lord. They fear that if they engage in psychological care, they will lose their religion. Your pastoral responsibility is to help the penitent understand and accept that a choice for good health is also a choice to accept God's will.

The first step in implementing this pastoral application is to help penitents understand that they are not primarily struggling with a spiritual problem, but a mental disorder. It is not their fault or their choice, but it is their reality. A wise confessor understands that penitents may not easily accept this news. One of the single biggest obstacles to helping penitents accept their scrupulosity and take the necessary steps to manage it is their own understanding of what they are dealing with. I cannot begin to relate how many good people have told me that scrupulosity is their "cross" and that is was "sent by Jesus." Others are convinced that they must somehow be possessed by the devil. Still others have different explanations, all of which are *false*.

Scrupulosity is rightly categorized as a disorder by medical doctors and psychologists and is recognized by the Church as an example of "diminished capacity" in the context of moral responsibility and culpability. (See *CCC* 1735; 1860.) It is a mental disorder that wreaks havoc on people's ability to decide about specific matters that are important to them.

Why is it essential for the priest confessor to help penitents understand and accept that OCD scrupulosity is a disorder? Because once the scrupulous realize that what they're suffering from is a mental disorder, they will be encouraged to apply the medical treatment essential to managing their pain. Gritting their teeth and "white-knuckling it" through life because they believe Jesus wants them to suffer in this manner is counterproductive. Looking for someone to expel their "demons" is also unhelpful. They need to embrace good, solid, well-thought-out and prescribed medical applications, supported by competent spiritual direction. So, to summarize, we must first correctly identify the scrupulous disorder and then take the necessary steps to engage scrupulous penitents in the healing process.

Accepting that they have a disorder does not eliminate the truth that there is a spiritual component to the suffering experienced by scrupulous people. They use a religious vocabulary as they struggle to express their suffering to the priest confessor who is trying to help them. Scrupulosity masquerades as a spiritual issue rather than a mental health issue. This is the cruelty of the scrupulous condition. It wraps itself in spiritual concepts to enable what it truly desires: anxiety, depression, shame, and, eventually, to isolate the scrupulous from everyone they care about.

People with scrupulosity are particularly effective in using big words that generate the anxiety this disorder thrives on; unfortunately, religion can be perceived as a system that's filled with big, complicated, and scary words. For example, scrupulous people quickly identify normal human sexual feelings as lust. They miscategorize questions that are essential for spiritual growth as blasphemy. For the scrupulous, everyday human conversations about life and relationships become calumny. And, of course, any deviation from the norm causes them worry and anxiety about validity and invalidity. The scrupulous constantly feel that they must engage in imagined restitution for what they are convinced they must be responsible for.

Upon hearing a penitent use big, scary words in confession, the priest confessor might be tempted to abandon good pastoral care because it seems to challenge the ordinary. Because so many components of the pastoral care and spiritual direction required to effectively manage scrupulosity are out of the realm of the ordinary, a more traditional or even rigid pastoral response might seem like the best choice.

The big, scary word that often gives a confessor pause in applying the necessary spiritual guidance is "relativism." The confessor must confront this fear and refuse to be paralyzed by it if he is to be effective in his pastoral care. In my pastoral experience, I have learned that there is relativism at work in moral theology. It is a real temptation, but it is not as prevalent as some people might make it seem. What is prevalent is the willingness of some theological commentators to carelessly use this loaded description, sow doubt, and insist that their more rigid approach is what is required. This is patently nonsense, but it is sometimes convincing.

When a scrupulous person moves past their fear of the big, scary words, new concerns or perceived worries come into focus. Perhaps the person is not guilty of a sin of commission, but what about the sins of omission? Sins of omission are never-ending; they are easily opened to exaggeration and misunderstanding; and they employ an unattainable standard. They provide a virtual playground for the scrupulous condition.

Even when a person with scrupulosity can acknowledge and accept each of the points I've outlined, the struggle is not over. The trump card that scrupulosity holds and plays is this: "Even if all of this is true for some people, you are the exception. Why would you want to risk condemnation because you are not sure?" This is a particularly compelling argument for a person who is already compromised by anxiety and fear.

Remember: everything the scrupulous mind generates is a

lie. There may be a kernel of truth in what it proposes, but the kernel is effectively minimized by all of the false components. For example, if people with scrupulosity engage in a compulsion or some kind of ritual action, they will feel better. That is the kernel of truth. What the scrupulous lie does not tell them is that the relief is not long-lasting; they will not find any real peace. In fact, their engagement in a compulsion is only a guarantee that the next obsessive action or thought will begin at the intensity at which the previous thought ended. In other words, it is progressive. It never resets to zero. It just gets more intense, stealthily becoming stronger in little increments so that the person who is suffering does not notice.

In the 1983 movie *WarGames*, starring Matthew Broderick and Ally Sheedy, a scene at the end of the movie makes an important point for this discussion. A massive and powerful computer, which is the central character of the movie, starts generating a continuous stream of questions, answers, and strategies in response to a problem. Each possible solution, although it initially looks promising and somewhat convincing, leads nowhere but to chaos. Just when it looks like things cannot get any more tense and that destruction is imminent, the computer suddenly stops its rampage and says, "Strange game. The only winning strategy is not to play."

And so it is. Not only in movies but also in life, particularly when scrupulosity is at work. The only winning strategy is not to play. Not to engage the compulsions or obsessions. Clearly, and with as much certitude as possible, identify the disorder for what it is. Refuse to engage with the terms it imposes. Manage it by learning and using the best practices, which can be effective, but do not play by the rules that scrupulosity requires. And, most certainly, do not believe the lies that scrupulosity generates about the individual person, his or her relationship with God, or his or her final destination (which the person fears is hell).

CHAPTER THREE

The Confessor as Surgeon

At first, this may sound "off the mark" for some, but the effective confessor who is dealing with a scrupulous penitent is not unlike a surgeon in the operating room.

When a surgeon is removing a tumor, he or she must remove the entire tumor for the operation to be a success. In addition to removing the tumor, the surgeon must remove some of the surrounding tissue to ensure that the disease does not spread. The surgeon cannot see with the naked eye where the healthy tissue begins but understands that he or she must remove a certain "margin" around the site of the tumor and that, in doing so, he or she is likely to remove some healthy tissue. To not remove the margin around the tumor is to risk the recurrence of the tumor, and so the operation would be pointless.

You cannot be a good surgeon if you are not fearless in the pursuit of a fully clean bill of health for the patient. You cannot compromise what you know to be necessary, because that is to risk failure.

The pastoral engagement between a scrupulous person and a skilled confessor or spiritual director needs the same kind of focus. The confessor or spiritual director must be fearless in applying the principles necessary to help the person manage his or her scrupulosity. He must be committed to doing what is necessary in just the same way that scrupulosity is committed to tormenting the soul it ravages. The confessor or spiritual director cannot compromise what he understands to be necessary for the scrupulous person's healing because that is to risk failure.

I did not always understand what was demanded from me as both confessor and spiritual director. I thought there might be a middle ground. I believed that I needed to have empathy and compassion, but I didn't understand or fully appreciate how persistently cruel and ruthless scrupulosity was. Indeed, I learned that, along with being compassionate and empathetic, I must apply the necessary behavior modifications to help the scrupulous person suppress what enables scrupulosity, which can include restricting religious practices and disciplines that trigger scrupulosity. This was very difficult for me to understand and accept. I felt at times like I was removing what was good and necessary, not unlike the surgeon who removes some healthy tissue to increase the chances of a full recovery.

I no longer need to be convinced. There is no middle ground. A confessor or spiritual director must fully and thoroughly apply the necessary religious and behavioral modifications to help the scrupulous person manage his or her disorder and, most importantly, experience the power of God's grace. To fulfill this commitment, the confessor or spiritual director must recognize and accept the context and the intersection of conflict with this understanding.

The Church calls all people to salvation, to repent and to believe in the gospel. The mission of the Church is to help all people of faith identify the points of weakness and failure in their lives, often identified as sins, so that they grow in the life of the Spirit. Throughout the centuries of fulfilling this mission, good men and women of faith—often saints but, more often, normal and ordinary people—have attempted specific disciplines and practices that helped them in their spiritual journey. As people of faith, we are grateful for what they have bequeathed to us.

All religious disciplines and practices that aid in proper awareness and identification of sin are useful. They help individual men and women become more cognizant of how they need to grow and develop and what they need to change in the process. That is the context. Here is the conflict: scrupulous people see sin everywhere. They do not need any help in identifying their failures and weaknesses. In fact, their scrupulosity consistently makes them aware of sin and routinely identifies the seriousness of their sins. By extension, scrupulosity also intensifies their peril when they feel they aren't doing enough about the seriousness of their perceived sins. What the Church intends as a help and guide does exactly the opposite for a scrupulous person: it magnifies his or her responsibility and the severity of his or her perceived sins, effectively condemning the person to the eternal punishment that scrupulosity promises because of his or her imperfections.

The context and conflict identify the pastoral dilemma that demands a response. How can a good priest confessor help free a person of the constant dread of eternal damnation and the burden this places upon the person while also affirming that every man and woman is sinful and needs God's forgiveness? The priest confessor must first remove the obstacles that prevent the person from hearing what is good and true so that he or she can hear the Good News of the gospel instead of the condemnation that his or her scrupulosity constantly announces.

Here is the ruthless application that is required for healing: remove, restrict, and contain every encounter with religious disciplines and practices that are primarily intended to remind a person that he or she has sinned. Replace condemnation with the experience of gratitude for God's grace and love. In the process, gently permit the grace of God to move a person away from condemnation into gospel living.

This surgical application requires you, as the confessor, to understand that the tumor—in this case, the scrupulosity that has contaminated the person who suffers from this torturous disorder—must be removed. You need to understand each part of what makes the scrupulous disorder effective on its path of destruction in the human person who is suffering. As discussed, this requires the surgical removal of even some of the healthy tissue around the margins, including the following religious practices, disciplines, and resources:

- The examination of conscience in any form
- Seeking reassurance and guidance from the *Catechism of the Catholic Church*
- Seeking reassurance and guidance from the *Code of Canon Law*
- Reading about the lives of the saints, particularly those who suffered from scrupulosity
- Consulting any resource that speaks of demonic possession
- The Divine Mercy Chaplet
- ANY repetitive prayer that can be counted. (This type of prayer opens the door to trying to be perfect and to pray with no distracting thoughts.)
- First Saturdays, scapulars, etc.
- Fasting and abstinence outside of the season of Lent. (Within Lent, the scrupulous person should practice fasting and abstinence only on the required days and not assume additional penances.)
- Promises or vows, unless publicly received by the competent authority
- Restitution, unless it is imposed by the priest as a condition for absolution

- The obligation for the Communion fast (dispensed)
- The sacrament of reconciliation (confession), unless it has been prepared for with a spiritual director/confessor and follows a strictly enforced schedule
- The formulation, "I am sorry for these sins and the sins of my past life, including..."
- Any question that begins with the words, "What if...?"

Each of these perfectly wonderful disciplines, practices, and resources are helpful and useful for a person who does not struggle with scrupulosity. However, for a person with the disorder, each of these is nothing more than a trigger for the obsessive and compulsive behavior that scrupulosity generates. They must not be engaged, no matter what.

It may be helpful in gaining an understanding of these necessary restrictions to consider the disease of alcoholism. No one would counsel or direct an alcoholic to abstain from drinking except at specific times or on certain occasions. It would be irresponsible to do so. Alcohol does not make exceptions. When the alcoholic engages in drinking, havoc follows—guaranteed. The same is true with scrupulosity. Once scrupulosity is triggered, you become a witness to the energy it generates and the obsessive and compulsive rituals it requires of the person until the disorder is—albeit only temporarily—satisfied. The person has no control. The only control is not to engage the disorder.

Confession and Canon Law

Individual and integral confession and absolution constitute the only ordinary means by which a member of the faithful conscious of grave sin is reconciled with God and the Church. Only physical or moral impossibility excuses from confession of this type; in such a case, reconciliation can be obtained by other means (*Code of Canon Law*, 960).

- Moral impossibility in general: This accounts for situations in which adhering to Church law would be too difficult/distressing for the penitent. In other words, fulfilling a particular law would cause more harm than good in the minds of those with grave conditions (scrupulosity/OCD, severe depression, etc.).
- Moral impossibility in the context of confession: This refers to the grave burden that making an integral confession (recounting mortal sins in number and kind) would place on the penitent. For example, when an integral confession causes the penitent to undergo agonizing recounting of sins and memories without being able to distinguish between what is truly a mortal sin and what is not mortally sinful, it would be difficult for the penitent to recognize God's grace of reconciliation at work. In this case, it would do more harm than good for the penitent to make a confession of this type.
- It is up to the judgment of the priest to determine other forms of reconciliation (Divine Mercy, rosary, certain prayers, time in prayer, etc.) if the person cannot make an individual confession.

- It's important to note that each Catholic is bound to confess only once a year. That gives time and space for a person to talk with his or her priest in advance, set an appointment, and make one individual and integral confession each year. But even this practice may take time for a scrupulous person to establish.

Once you understand how scrupulosity works and what it uses to generate pain and suffering, and you've determined that you are ready to proceed, I wish to assure you that you're making the correct pastoral choice. It will be difficult because it seems so out of the ordinary, and it is exactly what it seems to be: not at all common but highly destructive.

As priest and confessor, it may help to remind yourself of the theological foundation that supports the pastoral application you intend to engage: God has created his people to be saved, not to be condemned. And here is the remedial theological understanding of sin that you must understand to embrace this: simply put, God does not give up on his people as easily as we might seem to give up on God.

What gives me the confidence to be empathetic, compassionate, ruthless in the pastoral application of what is necessary to combat the scrupulous disorder, and, most of all, orthodox in the application of Catholic teaching and practice? The teaching of Jesus: "They tie up heavy burdens [hard to carry] and lay them on people's shoulders, but they will not lift a finger to move them" (Matthew 23:4). I'm also reminded of this Scripture passage, "Why, then, are you now putting God to the test by placing on the shoulders of the disciples a yoke that neither our ancestors nor we have been able to bear?" (Acts 15:10).

There is nothing unorthodox in this belief or in the required surgical removal of the tumor of scrupulosity from the lives of the men and women who suffer. The only difficulty is a lack of knowledge about how destructive scrupulosity is in the lives of those who suffer and their lack of access to the spiritual surgeons who can help them.

Pastoral note: Penitents will feel, and rightly so, that you are removing from their spiritual practices everything that is familiar to them. They may begin to panic and react with confusion. "If I cannot do any of these practices, then what can I do?" It is a good question. The answer is they must replace their old spiritual practices with a new one that will be helpful, not harmful.

Most people with scrupulosity have pushed aside any sense or awareness of gratitude, as they focus all their attention on being vigilant about failure, weakness, and sin. They need to rediscover gratefulness.

I suggest a simple, very helpful religious practice: each day, they spend some time thinking about *three* people, events, or experiences of that day for which they are grateful. They are asked merely to call these things to mind and express a simple prayer of thanks and gratitude to God. Nothing else is required; nothing is complicated.

Science informs us that the practice of gratefulness can profoundly change a person psychologically, emotionally, spiritually, and even physically. The *psychological* effects of a regular and deliberate practice of gratitude shifts attention from what's lacking or negative to what is present and good. Studies in positive psychology show that practicing gratitude increases overall happiness and life satisfaction, decreases symptoms of depression and anxiety, and fosters a more optimistic outlook.

The regular practice of gratitude also promotes *emotional* transformation. Practicing gratitude helps individuals become more resilient in the face of adversity; less prone to envy, resentment, or regret; and more appreciative of small, everyday blessings. Grateful people tend to be more empathetic and forgiving, have stronger relationships, and express appreciation more readily, improving communication and connection.

From a *spiritual* perspective, gratitude encourages humility before God and others, cultivates a sense of wonder and reverence, and deepens one's prayer life by shifting the focus to thanksgiving, not just prayers of petition and intercession.

Gratefulness is not simply a feeling; it is a discipline—a habit or spiritual practice that rewires how people see the world and respond to it. Over time, it can make a person more joyful, grounded, and compassionate.

The *gratefulness of the heart at prayer* is a deeply transformative disposition that shapes how a person relates to God, to him- or herself, and to the world. In Christian spirituality, especially within Catholic tradition, it is considered a vital posture of the soul, rooted in humility and love.

In the early 1970s and '80s, an often-recommended book for spiritual reading was *Prayer of the Heart* by Fr. George Maloney, SJ. His classic work on the Christian contemplative tradition encouraged readers to recognize that the gratefulness of the heart is more than saying "thank you"—it is a profound inner awareness and response to the goodness of God. It springs from recognizing life, salvation, and every blessing as unearned gifts from a loving Creator. This awareness leads to wonder at God's mercy and creation, trust in God's providence, even amid suffering, and joy in communion with God.

CHAPTER FOUR

Mortal Sin

Despite scrupulous penitents' great fear and the belief system that drives them, mortal sin is very difficult to commit—not impossible, but very difficult. This is my understanding and the perspective that gives me the courage to apply the necessary pastoral care when ministering to the scrupulous. It is not something you hear frequently about mortal sin, but, at the same time, it is central to our understanding of who we are as the people of God.

To reiterate, mortal sin is difficult for the average person in the pew to commit. I say this with the pastoral confidence generated by experience: a person in mortal sin is predictably somewhere other than in a church on any given Sunday. There are people in church who might find themselves in difficult pastoral situations, or people who are growing in their awareness of their need to rekindle their relationship with God, or people who are searching for relationship and meaning. Each of these are challenging pastoral realities, but to consign these people to the "bin of mortal sin" is pastorally insensitive.

It is almost impossible for a person with the scrupulous disorder to commit a mortal sin because of the "diminished capacity" that severely limits their ability to choose freely. This perspective is not a "golden ticket" to free a person from moral law or from living a Christian life. Most people who suffer from scrupulosity would gladly return their "golden ticket" to be free of the disorder.

I can almost see some readers flinching when they read that mortal sin is very difficult to commit. But let us stop, think about it, and remind ourselves of the teaching of the Church about mortal sin. This is not only necessary to understand my pastoral perspective, but it's also helpful for you as a confessor to proceed with confidence, knowing that you are on the correct path. Moreover, it is necessary for the scrupulous people, because they will surely ask you to explain what you're telling them, and it is best to be prepared for these questions.

For most readers, what I write here is a refresher, at least in the most basic understanding; however, some readers may find challenges in the interpretation that follows. But first, the traditional teaching:

Mortal sin in the traditional Catholic moral theological understanding refers to a grave violation of God's law that results in the loss of sanctifying grace and, if unrepented, leads to eternal separation from God (hell).

According to the *Catechism of the Catholic Church* (*CCC* 1855–1861), three conditions must be met for a sin to be considered mortal:

1. Grave matter: The action must be seriously wrong—for example: murder, adultery, theft, and the like. The Ten Commandments are often a reference point for grave matter.
2. Full knowledge: The person must know that what they are doing is gravely sinful and against the will of God.
3. Deliberate consent: The person must freely choose to commit the sin. It is not committed under force or grave psychological pressure.

Effects of Mortal Sin

- Loss of sanctifying grace in the soul
- Broken relationship with God
- Exclusion from heaven if not repented before death

Remedy for Mortal Sin

The ordinary means of forgiveness is through the sacrament of reconciliation (confession). Through true contrition, confession, and a firm purpose of amendment, a person will be restored to grace.

This is the traditional teaching of the Church about mortal sin, and it seems straightforward. However, a careful reading of the *Catechism of the Catholic Church*, paragraphs 1855–1861, reveals something that might be unexpected or, for that matter, even misunderstood. The *Catechism* reaffirms that mortal sin "is a radical possibility of human freedom" (*CCC* 1861), but the use of the term "mortal sin" is not as prevalent as a person might expect. In fact, it only appears in the following paragraphs, and nowhere else in the *Catechism*:

Mortal Sin in the *Catechism*

Paragraph(s)	Topic
1855–1857	Definition and conditions
1858–1861	Detailed explanation and effects
1861	Eternal consequences (hell)
1862–1864	Distinction from venial sin
1035	Mortal sin and hell
1455–1456	Need for confession
1493	Confession of grave sins required
2042	Church precept on confession

Another way of stating this is that mortal sin does not appear as a designation of responsibility where it might be expected, i.e., the consequence of missing Mass on Sunday, breaking the Eucharistic fast, eating meat on the Fridays in Lent, etc. In each of these examples, the *Catechism* prefers the designation of "grave" or "gravity." It could just as easily have used the designation "mortal," but it does not.

For some, this distinction might be characterized as "much ado about nothing," but that would be a mistake. The choice of wording in the *Catechism* is always deliberate; it is never casual. Thus, when a specific word is not chosen and another word is used in place of the word we might expect, there is a theological reason for the choice. This is worth paying attention to, and, for significant pastoral reasons, it is useful not to go on autopilot and say something like, "Well, grave sin and mortal sin are the same." No, not in all instances. That is not the understanding of the Church. It may be a shortcut, a quick way to summarize the teaching, but, as with all shortcuts, we can miss something. What is missing here is very important to understand in terms of pastoral care.

There is, in fact, a theological reason for the choice of language. It is important to first understand and then to pastorally apply this understanding where appropriate. In ministering to those who suffer with scrupulosity, the application provides the reasoning, theological context, and support for the pastoral decisions you need to make. The teaching of the Second Vatican Council (1962–1965) provides the pastoral direction.

The post–Vatican II Church placed greater emphasis on the subjective dimension of moral action—especially in the assessment of sin. There was a conscious and deliberative integration of moral theology and what might be understood as "personal subjectivity." This becomes very clear when referring to the *Code of Canon Law*, particularly when the 1917 *Code* is contrasted with the 1983 *Code*. To restate:

Mortal sin in theology requires:

1. Grave matter (objective)
2. Full knowledge
3. Deliberate consent

The 1983 *Code of Canon Law* more carefully reflects this by preferring terms like "grave sin" or "grave matter" that describe the objective component of the act without presuming personal culpability (which must be judged pastorally, not legally).

Canon law avoids declaring that someone has committed a mortal sin unless all conditions (including internal disposition) are clearly fulfilled—something not always possible in legal language.

Canon law, as ecclesiastical law, aims to provide universal and objective norms. The term "grave sin" is more canonically precise because it focuses on the external and verifiable action, leaving the internal disposition (full knowledge and consent) to pastoral judgment in the internal forum (e.g., confession).

The Second Vatican Council's emphasis on mercy, conscience, and pastoral accompaniment led to a shift in tone. The 1983 *Code* avoids the more judicial and moralistic tone sometimes found in the 1917 *Code*—for instance, "obstinate perseverance in manifest grave sin" (1983) versus "public sinner" or "mortal sin" (1917).

This helps avoid stigmatizing language, especially when the Church is addressing complex personal or moral situations (e.g., irregular marriages, mental illness, social pressures).

Though written later (1992), the *Catechism of the Catholic Church* (*CCC*), especially paragraphs 1854–1861, became a key theological reference that aligned closely with the 1983 *Code*.

- The *CCC* carefully explains that grave matter is a necessary component of mortal sin but doesn't assume culpability unless all conditions are met.
- This precision is reflected in the 1983 *Code*'s canonical terminology.

Terminology Comparison

Concept	***CIC* 1917**	***CIC* 1983**
Mortal sin	*Peccatum mortale* (used directly)	"Grave sin" or "grave matter"
Contrition	Often mentioned with mortal sin	Present, but with more pastoral nuance
Communion rules	Uses "mortal sin"	Uses "grave sin"

The 1917 *Code* frequently and clearly used "mortal sin" to describe moral conditions for the sacraments. On the other hand, the 1983 *Code*, while aligned theologically, tends to use "grave sin" to harmonize more closely with broader canonical language and the *Catechism of the Catholic Church*, which itself explains that grave matter + full knowledge + full consent = mortal sin.

The shift in language from explicitly using "mortal sin" in the 1917 *Code of Canon Law* to using "grave sin" or "grave matter" in the 1983 *Code* reflects deeper developments in theological understanding, pastoral sensitivity, and legal expression within the Church—especially influenced by the Second Vatican Council.

The shift from the term "mortal sin" to using "grave sin" in the 1983 *Code* is not a softening of doctrine, but rather a more theologically precise and pastorally responsible way of addressing sin in canon law. It maintains the seriousness of grave offenses while respecting the mystery of conscience, and it reflects a deeper integration between law, theology, and mercy.

Unfortunately, I must conclude this chapter with a statement that readers may not appreciate. I never imagined that such a statement would be necessary, but some may not find the argument I've presented about mortal sin convincing. They may regard it as suspect, a "watering down" of the authentic teaching of the Church, which they assume is the direct responsibility of the Second Vatican Council. For these priests, a return to the traditional understanding of the pre-Vatican II Church is essential, and all this talk about the subjective dimension of moral action is nothing more than a distraction.

If you are of this persuasion, there is really nothing I can say that will be of any use in your pastoral ministry, as most of these directives are based on a theology that takes the mystery of conscience very seriously and that reflects a deep integration between law, theology, and mercy. What I am championing is not "watered down" theology but rather is reflective of what the Church teaches.

Certainly, there are theological commentators, many of them active on social media, who believe we are engaged in theological warfare. The opinion of these commentators is that a few people might be harmed by a rigorous approach to theology—one that is more in line with the 1917 *Code* than the 1983 *Code*—but they are just "unfortunate yet necessary casualties." I find this position not only arrogant but also appalling. I might even go so far as to say that this positioning is a modern example of "blasphemy against the Holy Spirit" (See Matthew 12:31–32; Mark 3:28–29; Luke 12:10.), which has always been active in the Church. I consider it a modern example of blasphemy because the Holy Spirit most assuredly spoke with both teaching and traditional authority during the Second Vatican Council.

CHAPTER FIVE

The Confessor: Both Tested and Stretched

I hesitated to write chapter 3 on the priest as surgeon, but I had even more hesitation with this chapter. As priest confessor, you will be both tested and stretched in a manner that you might not expect when engaging in pastoral care with scrupulous people.

To be an effective confessor for the scrupulous, you must be willing to engage your own belief system and your own perceptions about what is required, what may be optional, and what can be set aside. Remember, we are not talking about ordinary pastoral care when it comes to ministering to the scrupulous; rather, we are talking about extraordinary pastoral care. I acknowledge that some of my brother priests have rarely considered that there is both ordinary and extraordinary pastoral care, so this may be difficult.

Ordinary pastoral care is what a priest is prepared for, and this is understandable. Most parishioners will never require anything more than good, solid, traditional pastoral care, which is tried and true. Thank God for these wonderful men, women, children, and families. But, seemingly more often in today's experience of the Church and ministry, the ordinary rubs up against the extraordinary with some regularity.

For example, ordinary pastoral care includes the typical ways in which pastors and the Church support the faithful in preparing for and fruitfully receiving the sacrament of reconciliation. This preparation includes catechesis, spiritual guidance, availability of the sacrament, and encouragement for ongoing conversion. A structured overview of ordinary pastoral care for this sacrament includes these familiar components.

1. Catechesis and Formation

- Initial instruction: Catechesis begins in childhood and includes teaching on:
- Sin (mortal and venial)
- Conscience and moral responsibility
- God's mercy and the meaning of repentance
- The matter/form and effects of the sacrament
- Ongoing formation: Adult faith formation and OCIA (Order of Christian Initiation of Adults) also include preparation for reconciliation.
- Parental involvement: For children, parents are the primary educators. Parishes often include them in the formation process.

2. Liturgical and Pastoral Practice

- Scheduled confession times: Parishes provide regular hours for the sacrament (e.g., Saturdays or before Mass).
- Penance services: Especially during Advent and Lent, communal penance services are held with individual confession and absolution.
- Private confession: Priests are available for confession by appointment or request.

3. Spiritual and Moral Guidance

- Examination of conscience: Ordinary pastoral care encourages examining the conscience before confession, guided by the Ten Commandments, beatitudes, or seven deadly sins.

- Encouragement of frequent confession: While once a year is the minimum (See the *Code of Canon Law*, 989.), frequent confession (monthly or more often) is encouraged for spiritual growth.
- Tender pastoral approach: Priests are instructed to be gentle and welcoming, especially to those who are hesitant or who are returning to confession after a long absence.

The Church in its wisdom, and through the experience of pastoral care over the centuries, has learned that, in addition to the ways people usually experience God's grace and love, there are experiences that are neither routine nor ordinary. Extraordinary pastoral care refers to situations in which the Church provides special or non-routine ministry to ensure that all the faithful have access to the grace of the sacrament, especially in times of urgent need, exceptional circumstances, or spiritual crisis. Two examples of this kind of pastoral care are:

- Irregular marital situations: People in complex marital situations may need careful guidance regarding this sacrament.
- Youth and first confession: This takes place before first Communion. Children must be properly disposed and understand the sacrament at their level.

A third example of extraordinary pastoral care is the subject we are discussing: the person who is struggling with scrupulosity. It is extraordinary pastoral care because it presents an urgent need. The disorder generates exceptional circumstances that masquerade as normal and essential. The disorder provokes an ongoing spiritual crisis.

With the emphasis of both preaching and catechesis on the reception of the sacrament of reconciliation, particularly in the form of individual confession, going to confession is perceived as ordinary pastoral practice. Scrupulous people respond to this emphasis, and, as a result, many people who suffer from the disorder routinely seek individual confession, believing this is the minimum of what is required of them.

What compels the scrupulous to seek reconciliation through confession is not an informed conscience or a sense of moral responsibility, but an exaggerated sense of condemnation. They are acting out compulsions and obsessions. They receive the usual guidance and directives, then filter them through their disorder, which insists that confession is necessary. They truly don't understand that confession is neither helpful nor healthy for them. A person without scrupulosity may benefit from a renewed emphasis on participating in confession, but a scrupulous person will not.

The exceptional circumstance manifested by the OCD scrupulous ritual is that scrupulous people sincerely believe they are in a state of mortal sin and need immediate forgiveness. This belief is intensified by what they hear from the pulpit or on social media. They misinterpret that the normal and essential response to mortal sin for a practicing Catholic is to seek the sacrament of reconciliation as soon as possible. To not receive the sacrament is to risk dying in a state of mortal sin and thus eternal damnation. Again, the sacrament is a necessary spiritual practice for a person without scrupulosity. For a scrupulous person, however, this practice is not rooted in a healthy response to God's grace, but in fear. The scrupulous person has an exaggerated fear and hypersensitivity to perceived moral feelings—further intensified by real feelings of guilt, shame, and anxiety—which he or she misinterprets as a confirmation that sin is indeed present.

Here is where the confessor's intervention is essential. At the same time, it may also be the place where the confessor is tested and stretched.

When you, as confessor, encounter a person in confession who is fully engaged in the ritual generated by OCD scrupulosity, you must listen carefully. Try not to become distracted by the specific words the person uses and the long, detailed explanations. Rather, pay close attention to the feelings the person is expressing, using the language of sin to describe the reality of what he or she is experiencing. No matter how it sounds to you—sincere and sometimes even convincing—remember this: the feelings are real, but the person's interpretation of what the feelings mean is false. Big words and complex explanations do not indicate grave sin; rather, they indicate the depth of the fear, anxiety, and shame that the person is feeling.

Your pastoral response to the scrupulous ritual should not be reassurance. You should not discuss the concept of sin on any level. You most certainly should not say something like, "That is not a sin." Every fiber of your being might want to respond to the person's pain and suffering by trying to calm, clarify, or catechize. But knowledge is not helpful at this point; this is not a teaching moment. Limit your pastoral counsel to the person's reality, not the masquerade. You have not witnessed a confession of sin. You have witnessed a demonstration of true mental anguish and suffering. Your pastoral counsel should focus on the suffering, not on the details.

An appropriate response might be something like this:

I have heard your sincere confession. I am satisfied that you are being totally honest. I have no questions to ask you. I have no need for further details. I know you are being completely vulnerable and are not deliberately hiding anything.

Jesus has accepted your confession and forgives you. Even more important, Jesus loves you, exactly as you are, at this moment in time. He is well pleased.

To celebrate the forgiveness that Jesus gives to you in this sacrament, please pray three Hail Marys. They do not have to be perfect; it is enough that you try to pray them. I will now give you absolution. Please pay attention to the fact that I am praying every word of the Prayer of Absolution exactly as it is required:

God, the Father of mercies, through the death and resurrection of his Son has reconciled the world to himself and poured out the Holy Spirit for the forgiveness of sins; through the ministry of the Church may God grant you pardon and peace, and I absolve you from your sins in the name of the Father, (+) and of the Son, and of the Holy Spirit.

At first glance, this formulation may look and sound very laborious. It is, but it is intended to cover almost every one of the penitent's fears and doubts. When the person leaves the confessional, it may give him or her the support and encouragement that he or she needs, at least for a few minutes. No formula is perfect, but we do know what *not* to do, and that is anything that provides reassurance, engages details, acknowledges the person's fear of sin, and the like.

As a confessor, you might feel tested and stretched by responding to the penitent in this way. You probably will feel that you could have said something more or clarified something better. Perhaps you will think you can offer an explanation that will be exactly what the penitent needs. I am sorry to disappoint you, but responding to the scrupulous penitent in the way that I've outlined here is what is required and necessary.

When you respond in this very pastoral manner, with an understanding of the person's suffering, you are an instrument of God's healing grace, not a pawn of the scrupulous disorder. You are refusing to engage scrupulosity in a way that energizes and confirms the pain it causes. You are instead choosing to offer the scrupulous person a path to the real possibility of healing and wholeness. You are manifestly trusting not in your own skills and talents, but rather in the power of the Holy Spirit that is present in the sacrament.

The hope that emerges from this kind of response is that the scrupulous person will seek the spiritual direction and pastoral care that he or she needs. You have identified yourself as someone who is willing to help him or her. It may take some time before the person asks for help. Nevertheless, you have significantly increased the likelihood that he or she will eventually ask for help.

It is unlikely that the description and formulation I have provided here will be all that is required, and that you and the scrupulous penitent will seamlessly move on to the next step in pastoral care right away. You will probably need to repeat this process numerous times. It is important that, each time, you return to the formulation I've provided and do not stray from the boundaries it creates. If this is the only result of your effort, regard it as the expression of God's grace. Do not judge the efficacy of God's grace. Let all things unfold in God's time. At the same time, the penitent may respond in a positive way sooner than you think. The scrupulous person sincerely wants to be healed and to live freely.

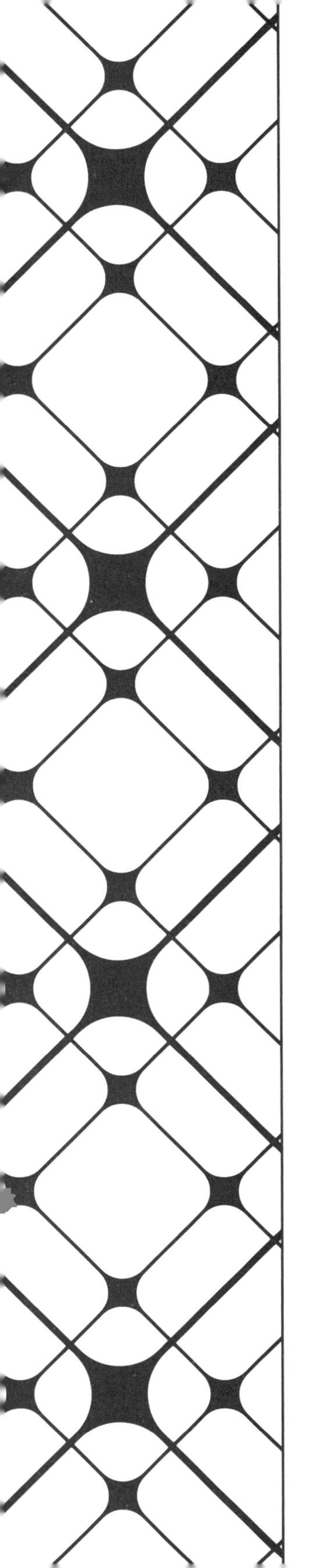

CHAPTER SIX

Spiritual Direction for the Scrupulous Person

When a scrupulous penitent who experiences your pastoral care in the confessional takes the next step and seeks spiritual direction from you, you must prepare yourself for the encounter that you have enabled.

In the first session of spiritual direction, set the tone for what will unfold. It is not a time for them to ask a litany of questions, although this is very easy to fall into. Do not let the directee lead the conversation; as spiritual director, you set the parameters of the conversation. Listen to the directee's concerns, of course, but also steer the person to consider the truth that will help him or her instead of the fear and anxiety that weakens him or her.

- Ask the person to talk about his or her upbringing and family. Listen for any mention of a family member who suffered from anxiety, depression, or other mental illness.
- Ask about the person's current living situation. Does the person live with or regularly engage with people, or does he or she live an isolated life?
- Ask if the person has had any therapy or is taking prescription medication. If so, how has it helped?
- Ask the person to share with you his or her current spiritual practice, including how often he or she goes to confession and holy Communion?
- Does the person pray memorized prayers? Is he or she committed to these particular prayers, or does he or she feel free to pray different prayers each day?
- Is the person concerned with achieving perceived perfection in his or her prayers, saying them repeatedly until they are "correct"?

- Where does the person go for reassurance and answers to questions? Social media? The *Catechism* or the *Code of Canon Law*? How much time does he or she spend in doing this?

Note: *You must clearly explain to the person that these resources are not meant to be used for reassurance and should be avoided by people with scrupulosity. Further, few laypeople have the training to properly use these resources as they are intended.*

Somewhere in the conversation, compliment the person on his or her response to the grace of God working in his or her life. Despite the struggles and suffering, this person has nevertheless remained open to the grace of God. This is a great gift, and he or she has freely chosen to respond to that gift (for example, by seeking spiritual direction, counseling, etc.). God's grace and the person's continual response to that grace will help him or her manage the disorder going forward.

Finally, review with the person what he or she has learned in this first session. Discuss and determine whether he or she wants to continue spiritual direction. If so, you have some conditions that he or she will need to meet the next session. The scrupulous person must:

1. Eliminate all OCD triggers, including researching, reading books, and visiting social media for reassurance, as well as asking other people for advice. This means a radical readjustment of the person's spiritual practice and discipline.
2. Eliminate any kind of examination of conscience.
3. Stop going to confession. The person will be able to go to confession again in the future, but only when he or she is prepared to celebrate it—when it is not a compulsion or obsession.

4. Receive holy Communion no matter how he or she feels. No exception.

More than likely, the person will ask you where all these conditions come from and why he or she has never heard any of this from a priest or spiritual director before. The answer is that this is *orthodox* Catholic teaching. The person has not heard this before because, until now, he or she has not talked to a priest or spiritual director who has spoken to him or her from the perspective of helping a person with scrupulosity.

Conclude the session by thanking the person for cooperating with God's grace. Ask him or her to try to implement your conditions. If he or she fails, it is not a disaster; just start again. It will take time and patience, but he or she will get there. The scrupulous person can learn to manage the disorder.

During the first meeting, you accomplished quite a bit, and so did the directee.

Make a follow-up appointment in five to seven weeks. This gives the person a sufficient amount of time to implement and practice what you have directed him or her to do.

Going Forward: Session Two and Beyond

At your next meeting with the directee, review the progress that he or she is making, encourage him or her to keep trying, and remind the person that this disorder is difficult to manage. Whenever the directee asks a question—and he or she will ask many of them—*never* answer it. Review his or her decision-making process. It is this person's conscience, not yours. The directee needs to practice the skills that will help him or her manage the disorder. If you answer those questions, you are not helping the person moving forward.

In every situation possible, *widen the scrupulous person's perspective and context.* Remind the person that life is not a series of rules and obligations; it is meant to be lived, and living means there will be successes, failures, and a lot of middle ground. Life is not a series of traps that God has set to condemn him or her.

Do not engage the scrupulous person in a conversation about sin. Remember, people with scrupulosity are masters on this topic, because it is what concerns them the most, and you are an apprentice. If you participate in a conversation about sin, you will not be helping the person. This person will not be satisfied until you respond with the exact answer he or she wants to hear. It is a fool's errand.

Remember, *all* questions from someone with scrupulosity are loaded questions, and you are doomed if you think you can provide an answer. You cannot. He or she is not trying to trick you or set you up for failure—it is the OCD at work.

Help the person understand that the fertile ground of OCD is the *past* and the *future.* OCD cannot exist in the *present moment.* If the person wants to manage his or her scrupulosity, he or she must focus on and pay attention to the *present,* where there is no energy to fuel the scrupulous condition. (Mindfulness practices are very important and useful. See chapter 7.)

God is the *Eternal Now.* God does not have a concern about the directee's past and/or future. It is already known fully to God, just as this person is. He has already made a judgment about the person, and that is the *judgment of love.* Anything that robs the directee of the present and life-giving experience of God's love is OCD. We will explore this further in the next chapter.

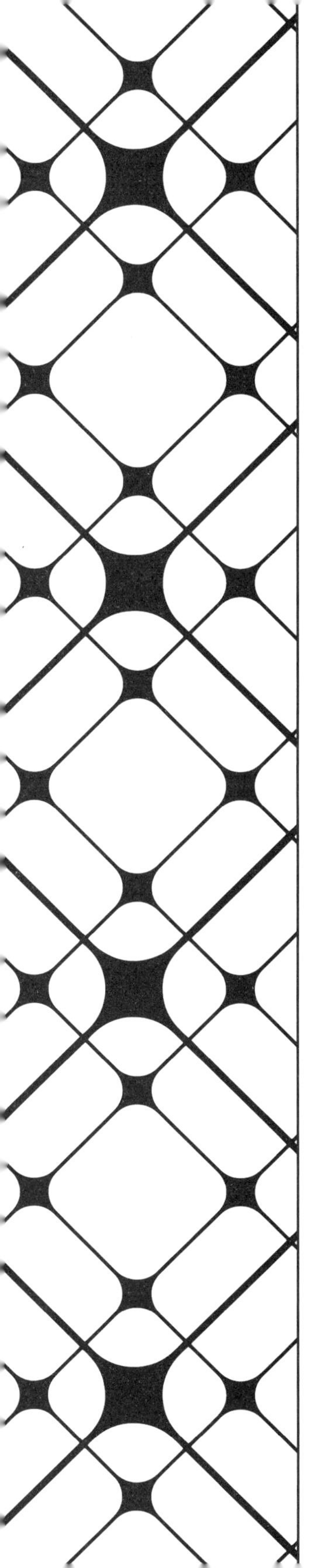

CHAPTER SEVEN

The Eternal Now

In spiritual direction, I often remind the scrupulous person of a simple truth: scrupulosity thrives only in the future or in the past; it cannot thrive in the present moment. In the present, there is no oxygen to energize the anxiety (or whatever is the person's dominant feeling). This may seem obvious, but it is not. OCD rumination—the fear of the past or the concern for the future—is highly manipulated, greatly exaggerated, seemingly truthful, and so powerful as to make it believable, all the while discarding the present moment as the healthy choice.

From a non-spiritual perspective, trying to enter the present moment and focus one's attention and concern on that moment is often identified as *mindfulness*. It can be helpful to understand mindfulness in this manner, but I believe it to be incomplete because it can sound like a gimmick or perhaps something "new age" or from a different religious practice. This is unfortunate, because trying to live in the present moment is very spiritual. It is the core principle of a contemplative religious practice, a healthy practice that is fueled by grace.

The present moment is also something of the divine—a real connection between divinity and humanity. In fact, the present moment is the dwelling place of God. God is in the present moment. God *is* the present moment. God is the Eternal Now. When we say that God is the Eternal Now, we mean that God is timeless. In God, there is no future and no past; there is only the present. At the same time—and this is where the concept stretches the human mind and understanding—all the past and all the future, in their entirety, are in the Eternal Now. For divinity, it simply *is*. For humanity, it is simply unknown—a mystery, if you will. It cannot be understood; it must simply be accepted and hopefully celebrated.

From a Christian perspective, when the Second Person of the Holy Trinity became a human being, he freely entered time and assumed a past and a future, all the while living a present reality in his day-to-day life. This is what Scripture means when it proclaims that Jesus became like us in all things but sin. (See Hebrews 4:15.) Jesus set aside, so to speak, the Eternal Now and freely embraced the full experience of humanity. How this happened is beyond our understanding. That it did happen is the core belief of Christian faith and life.

When fueled by our scrupulosity, we resist the present moment and drown ourselves in either the future or the past, effectively depriving ourselves of our connection with God. This deprivation is what makes us fearful, anxious, shameful, and worried. It is what fuels the spiraling way of thinking and perceived logic of the disorder. If, on the other hand, we strive to enter the present moment, we are no longer deprived of the presence of God. We hear the words of God, who knows all things, who knows our entire story, when he says to us, "You are my beloved, in whom I am well pleased." There can be no other blessing, no other judgment, no other reality.

We cannot earn this blessing. It comes to us, unmerited, from a generous God. We can, however, learn to celebrate it and live it each day. In fact, it becomes our motivation to do good and to choose what is right—not out of fear, but out of love.

For a person who strives to live in the present moment, the prayer of St. Paul the Apostle is descriptive of our lived reality:

> *Love is patient, love is kind. It is not jealous, [love] is not pompous, it is not inflated, it is not rude, it does not seek its own interests, it is not quick-tempered, it does not brood*

over injury, it does not rejoice over wrongdoing but rejoices with the truth. It bears all things, believes all things, hopes all things, endures all things. Love never fails.

1 Corinthians 13:4-8a

The words of the apostle effectively confront the garbage thinking that is generated by the scrupulous disorder and claim the rightful birthright of each child of God. If we want to both hear and experience these words of power and truth, we need to look no further than the present moment, the Eternal Now.

Whenever I hear a condemning or judgmental word in my head, I do not react to it; instead, I remind myself of the truth of who I am as a child of God. Whenever I encounter so-called preachers and teachers of the word of God on social media who peddle nonsense, conditions, rules, and regulations, and who "tie up heavy burdens [hard to carry] and lay them on people's shoulders, but...will not lift a finger to move them" (Matthew 23:4), I remind myself that I am blessed—not cursed.

Every scrupulous person understands both compulsion and obsessiveness. Every scrupulous person understands the feeling of helplessness when he or she is trapped in uncompromising rituals that are generated by their scrupulous condition. I know that each person who suffers with this terrible disorder understands that scrupulosity generates lies. Scrupulosity is incapable of telling the truth. The only truthful thing about scrupulosity is that it is not true. It is never true; it is always dishonest.

No matter how helpless and hopeless a person might feel, there is real hope. I believe that each of you also understands that we cannot effectively combat the disorder in either the future or in the past, in the endless questions asked by the scrupulous, or in the details that scrupulosity demands. It is only in the present moment, safe in the arms and the heart of the Eternal Now, that the scrupulous may find peace, comfort, and joy.

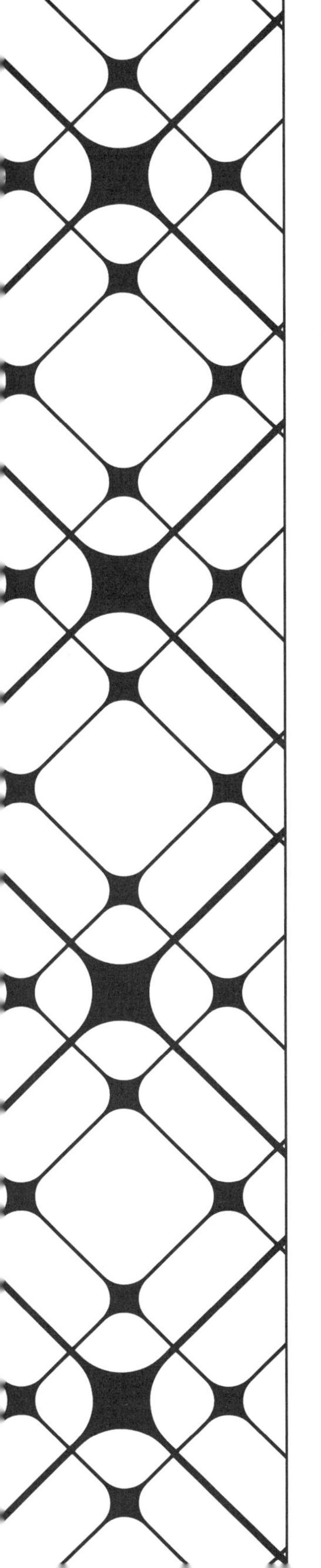

CHAPTER EIGHT

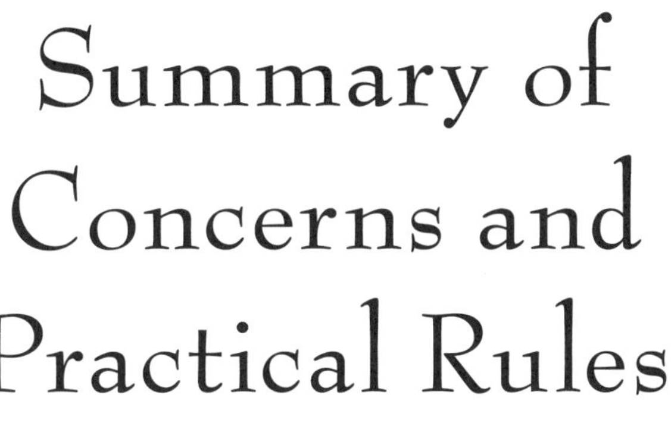

Summary of Concerns and Practical Rules

Following is a list of the most common concerns of scrupulous people and the practical rules I frequently reference when ministering to people with scrupulosity. The list is hardly exhaustive, but it does indicate some common themes that you will often experience. My perspective is not the only perspective, but I offer each of the following concerns and rules in the hopes that it will be a helpful resource to aid you in your pastoral response.

A general rule for directing the scrupulous person is to try and unpack his or her understanding or interpretation of a point, practice, or discipline ***before*** *you offer commentary or engage the person in conversation.* ***Never*** *presume that you understand what the person is referring to; you do not. You must learn what the person means; you must not advise him or her about a situation based on what you think they mean.*

Expressed Concerns

Fraternal correction: Some scrupulous people feel that they need to correct other people and inform them that their behavior is wrong. The consistent direction provided by the directors of Scrupulous Anonymous over the years is that a scrupulous person should never attempt to give advice to another person. The only exception is if the scrupulous person is directly responsible for providing direction, for example, to a minor child (but not an adult child); in this case, he or she should be very selective.

Sexuality: All questions about sexuality and attempts to define sexual expressions, limits, and parameters should be redirected. You should stress repeatedly that sexuality is complex and nuanced. The Church teaches that it is serious, yes, but the moral tradition of the Church also teaches care and compassion and resists a rush to judgment. Respect, mutual boundaries, and honesty in relationships are important, but attempts to zero in on a particular sexual act, expression, or fear are never helpful and will only trigger more questions and more anxiety.

Nudity is not a sin. Sexual feelings are not sinful. Impure thoughts are natural. A person does not control his or her thoughts. There is no set criteria for "entertaining thoughts" in which they morph from venial sins to mortal sins. A person can feel sexual with a certain smell or the feeling of a cool breeze, for example. No one controls these things, and their interpretation should not automatically default to serious sin. Sex should not be feared or be a cause of anxiety. Encourage the scrupulous person to keep it in context and presume that sex is a gift, not the shameful or guilt-inducing act that their OCD prefers.

Restitution: Once a person starts going down the path of trying to determine restitution, it becomes overwhelming quickly. It's a trap; a rabbit hole. Scrupulous people should avoid at all costs considering any type of restitution. From a moral point of view, the working presumption is that restitution is rarely, if ever, required. It should be considered *only* if the priest confessor imposes it as a condition of absolution. It is not the scrupulous person's duty to determine restitution.

Reconciliation: Forgiveness can be experienced through an Act of Contrition, receiving holy Communion, and celebrating the sacrament of anointing. These are the ordinary ways in which a scrupulous person can receive and celebrate reconciliation. The sacrament of reconciliation is required only if a person is in mortal sin. The scrupulous person is not in mortal sin, even though they may experience the fear of mortal sin. It is not the same thing.

Sabbath rest: This is another rabbit hole. It is best to steer a scrupulous person completely away from trying to dissect and determine what he or she can do or cannot do on a Sunday. The concept of entertainment, relaxation, living in a secular society where not everyone follows the same religious path—all of these details are just confusing to someone with scrupulosity. The simplest answer is to inform the person that he or she should not apply their understanding/anxiety/fears to the Sabbath and should just go with the flow.

Prayers before meals: Such prayers are not a requirement; they are an optional spiritual practice.

Dispensation: Each person has the right—indeed, the obligation—to determine his or her own healthy and integrated spiritual practice; to participate when he or can and when it is helpful, and to decline to *participate* when it is not. A person can decide; that's the way it is. Because this is difficult for scrupulous people, the best advice for them is to err on the side of generosity and compassion, not to follow the strictest possible interpretation.

Near-occasion of sin: This is a very slippery slope. Yes, there are occasions that a person might need to avoid because they have "trouble written all over them." This is hopefully a lesson learned early in life from parental guidance. However, one does not need to be vigilant at all times, always on the lookout for the near-occasion of sin. Ordinary life does not usually encounter extraordinary temptation. One has to look for it.

Practical Rules

Admittedly, as a direct result of my years of ministry with scrupulous people, I am absolutely ruthless in applying what is required to manage scrupulosity. I will not compromise in applying the necessary pastoral remedy. I have patience and understanding for the many scrupulous people I've worked with, who are often crippled by the doubts they experience daily. I urge and practice compassion and generosity, but I will not compromise.

When a person is struggling with OCD scrupulosity, the trigger is the content that demands the person's attention. OCD does not have any loyalty to the content; it cares only for the anxiety the content produces. Any attempt by the scrupulous person to answer the many questions generated by the content is a total and complete waste of time. My practical rules for people with scrupulosity, and how I communicate these rules to them, include the following:

Examination of conscience: If you experience stress, anxiety, doubt and confusion when you are examining your conscience, stop it. You cannot engage in this spiritual practice. Period. No exception.

Confession: If you are going to confession numerous times a week, or even numerous times a day, stop it; this is not necessary or required. This is not spirituality or spiritual practice; it is OCD. You are not experiencing grace, you are becoming exhausted and overwhelmed by your OCD.

Forgotten details: If you have finished your confession and remember some detail that you believe you should have mentioned, stop it. It is a lie. This content is not your friend; it is OCD. Refuse to consider it. Move on. Walk away. What is done is done; it is enough, and nothing more is required.

Holy Communion: If you experience scrupulosity when you are standing in the Communion line and are convinced that you are in a state of sin and cannot receive holy Communion, stop it. Receive holy Communion no matter what you feel.

Mortal or venial sins: If you are struggling to determine whether something is a grave, or mortal, sin or a venial sin, stop it. This is your scrupulosity wreaking havoc within you. Your diminished capacity to freely choose, which routinely defaults to the most serious sin and claims responsibility for committing this sin, is scrupulosity at work.

Prayer: If you find yourself endlessly repeating prayers to make them "perfect," stop the prayers. It is enough that you are sitting or kneeling in the sacred space of prayer. Be silent and refuse to engage the trigger. You do not need words to pray. It is enough that you are present.

Permissions: If you find yourself frozen in place, believing that you need permission from God to make a move, stop it. Force yourself to walk away and continue what you were doing. Refuse to ask for permission. It is not God who requires it; it is your OCD, and it is a lie.

Impulsive thoughts: If you have an impulsive thought and it disgusts you, admit that you are disgusted and then stop thinking about it. There is no need to review it, digest it, and figure out the details. There is certainly no need to determine if you "entertained" it. You do not entertain bad thoughts; your OCD does, not you.

Sexual feelings: If you have a sexual feeing, even arousal, thank God for the fact that you are alive and healthy. Stop condemning yourself. Stop trying to figure out if you caused it. Stop it.

Sabbath rest: If you find yourself constantly wondering what is acceptable and what is not acceptable as an activity on a Sunday, stop it. This is not spiritual. This is a trigger for OCD and anxiety.

Signs from God: If you hear a voice or see a sign that makes you think God is talking to you and directing you to act in a specific manner, stop it. Your OCD makes it impossible to trust that the voice you hear is the voice of God. It is your OCD lying to you and causing you stress and anxiety.

Content is not a friend for the scrupulous person; it is the trigger for anxiety. Content is also the trigger for compulsive and obsessive thinking. Content makes the scrupulous person ruminate about the past and fear, even dread, the future. The scrupulous person must be encouraged to stop looking for clarification, reassurance, and accumulating more content. The scrupulous person must close the *Catechism*. Hide the *Code of Canon Law*. Stop listening to comments on social media made by people who are clueless about scrupulosity or who tend to dismiss mental illness and blame it on demons. A scrupulous person does not need this content. He or she does not need to be triggered in this manner.

With the help of a good confessor/spiritual director, scrupulous people can learn to be confident in their own disciplined and practiced decisions. First, they must understand the necessity of seeking and finding a good spiritual director and/or confessor. They can include their significant others and loved ones in at least a basic awareness of their struggles. All of this is good and necessary. But scrupulous people must also stop looking for and accumulating content—they must starve the beast and isolate the content that triggers their suffering.

APPENDIX A

When Confession Is Necessary

A Sample Formula

Preparing a scrupulous person for the sacrament of reconciliation does not have to be a burden or an exhausting task. It is quite simple, as long as the penitent sticks to the basics of what is required and necessary. The person should remember that there is tremendous grace in simply presenting him- or herself for the sacrament and admitting that he or she is a sinner in need of God's grace. The person shouldn't minimize this action and response. It is powerful, in and of itself. Everything else that follows is understood as a celebration of God's grace; the details of his saving action on the penitent's behalf. It is not a test. It is not a burden. There is no such thing as "passing" or "failing." It is an encounter with Jesus, and it should be acknowledged and celebrated as such.

The formula that follows has been repeatedly helpful in enabling scrupulous people to celebrate the sacrament of reconciliation without risking major triggers that will encourage obsessive or compulsive ritual responses.

Bless me Father, for I have sinned. I am scrupulous. I am under the direction of a spiritual director who is helping me with my scrupulosity. I am following my spiritual director's instruction in this confession. I am aware that I am a sinner. I know and understand that I need God's mercy, and I desire to celebrate God's forgiveness in this sacrament. I know with certitude that I have sinned. (At this time, confess, in a very general manner, clear and certain sins with ***no detail*** *and* ***no explanation****.) I am sorry for these sins and all of my sins, and I ask for penance and absolution from you.*

Specific Advice

- Inform the penitent that most priests will gratefully accept this form of confession, give him or her a penance, and offer him or her absolution.
- As a confessor, if you do not accept this form of confession, please do not insist on more details or further information. In short, end the confession. Let the scrupulous person seek compassionate pastoral care elsewhere.

APPENDIX B

The Saints on Obedience to Your Confessor

Several Catholic saints strongly emphasized the importance of obeying one's confessor/spiritual director, seeing this obedience as a path to humility, discernment, and holiness. Here are some key examples and insights:

Saint Teresa of Ávila

"The safest course in these things is to declare, without fail, the whole state of the soul, together with the graces our Lord gives me, to a confessor who is learned, and obey him."

The Life of Saint Teresa of Jesus,
Chapter 24

Teresa stressed that even if the director errs, God will reward the obedience, and the soul will not be harmed. Obedience is a shield against illusion in prayer.

Saint John of the Cross

"The virtuous soul that is alone and without a master is like a lone burning coal; it will grow colder rather than hotter."

Sayings of Light and Love, 7

A spiritual person, no matter how virtuous, benefits from the guidance of a wise spiritual director.

Saint Francis de Sales

"'Choose one among a thousand,' Ávila says—and I say among ten thousand... when you have found [a good spiritual director]...seek no more but go on simply, humbly, and trustfully."

Introduction to the Devout Life, **Part I, Chapter 4**

Constancy is key. Frequent changes of spiritual director cause instability; one trusted guide ensures steady growth.

Saint Ignatius of Loyola

"Our enemy may also be compared in his manner of acting to a false lover.... He wants his words and solicitations kept secret."

The Spiritual Exercises, **Rules for Discernment, Week 1, Rule 13**

Keeping secrets from a spiritual director opens the door to temptation; openness and obedience close it. In the *Spiritual Exercises,* Ignatius insists that retreatants reveal everything to the director.

Saint Alphonsus Liguori

"Even when it is doubtful whether the object of a precept is conformable to the law of God...a religious is bound to obey; and that in obeying [he or she] is certain of not sinning, and of even pleasing God."

***The True Spouse of Jesus Christ,* Chapter 7**

Alphonsus considered obedience to a spiritual director to be a sign of humility and a guarantee of God's blessing, even if human judgment errs.

Summary of Principles

Obedience to a spiritual director/confessor is not blind submission but a humble trust in God's guidance through the Church and its ministers. It guards against deception, fosters humility, and leads to holiness.

In choosing and interacting with a spiritual director, the scrupulous person should implement the following steps:

1. **Pray for discernment:** Before choosing a director, the person should look for someone grounded in faith and experienced in spiritual guidance.
2. **Be transparent:** Share joys, struggles, and temptations openly with his or her director.
3. **Avoid "director shopping":** Once the person has chosen a spiritual director, he or she should not change directors unless it becomes necessary for serious reasons.

4. **Trust but verify:** If advice contradicts Church teaching, the person should seek clarification—obedience is not absolute.
5. **Act promptly on guidance:** Delayed obedience often weakens its fruit.
6. **Unite obedience with faith:** The person should view his or her director as God's instrument for growth, not as a mere advisor.

Very often, it is the demonstrated willingness of people with scrupulosity to follow the direction of the saints that enables their positive response to your direction. It is almost like the teaching of the saints is perceived as a stamp of approval from the heavenly Host or, to use secular terminology from the 1950s and '60s, the "*Good Housekeeping* Seal of Approval." Regardless, the important thing is that it enables scrupulous people to respond and often strengthens their response when they are struggling with OCD triggers.

APPENDIX C

Ten Commandments for the Scrupulous

Preamble: In the 1960s, when Father Don Miller, CSsR, penned the original commandments, he understood scrupulosity in the traditional manner: as a "manifestation of the tender conscience." He believed the best treatment was good catechetical advice and direction from a skilled confessor.

Today we understand that scrupulosity can be a tender conscience, but it may also be a form of obsessive-compulsive disorder (OCD) with a religious manifestation. As a disorder, and not a question of conscience or religious formation, catechetical formation will have little or no impact on a person with OCD-based scrupulosity. People with scrupulosity think and study about sin repeatedly, to little or no avail. You cannot think or study your way out of OCD.

- Commandments 1 through 4 focus on the sacrament of reconciliation.
- Commandments 5 and 6 focus on behaviors and uncontrolled thoughts that ignite concerns about sacrilege and/or disrespect for God and his saints. Both commandments address the fear of losing control or risking "safety."
- Commandments 7 and 8 focus on doubt, specifically the issues of resisting your confessor's directives and confusion about obligations.
- Commandments 9 and 10 address the seemingly constant fear experienced by people with scrupulosity and the need to put individual trust in Jesus, who is the way, the truth, and the life.

First Commandment

Without exception, you shall not confess sins you have already confessed.

The most persistent experience of people with scrupulosity is doubt accompanied by never-ending anxiety: "Have I thoroughly and completely confessed my sins?" That's why scrupulosity is called the "doubting disease." Doubt-generated anxiety deprives us of the peace of Christ, our birthright through grace.

When doubt and/or anxiety are removed from the equation, the scrupulosity—although not healed—is significantly reduced.

Resisting the urge to confess doubtful sin or sins you've already confessed is a pastoral remedy that will bring peace. When you refuse to engage the feeling of doubt and thereby resist the urge to animate and energize your scrupulosity, the wave of anxiety passes over you—and you can enjoy the peace that inevitably occurs. Yes, it is difficult. Yes, it is fearsome. Yes, it takes practice. But it can be achieved, and the result is gratifying.

Second Commandment

You shall confess only sins that are clear and certain.

This commandment gets to the heart of the scrupulosity struggle with its directive to accept that doubtful sins don't count. You needn't confess something that does not clearly and certainly exist. In fact, it's harmful to confess that which is doubtful. Such a practice is not at all helpful and must be resisted.

I can almost hear some of you saying, "I'm not sure whether I doubt that I sinned or that I'm trying to fool myself into believing that I'm doubting I sinned." Simply having that thought demonstrates your doubt. That's where this commandment comes into play: You shall confess only sins that are clear and certain.

Many people with scrupulosity think that people who don't have scrupulosity are somehow completely free of doubt. But it's a myth that a healthy state of mind exists in which everything is clear, black and white, and knowable without any sense of struggle. Some people do live in such a state, but they have a condition that's just as problematic as OCD.

Doubt is natural and normal. It's not an indication of sinfulness—it's the normal experience of being a human person, who is incomplete and often imperfect, in short, exactly as God as created you.

This second commandment also encourages clear and certain confession. The penitent states his or her sinfulness clearly and without hesitation, excuse, or innumerable details.

If the confessor is unsure of what you're clearly confessing, it is his responsibility to ask for clarification. If he doesn't ask for clarification, accept that you have been clearly and certainly understood. Do not take on a role that is not yours.

Third Commandment

You shall not repeat your penance or any of the words of your penance after confession—for any reason.

Father Don Miller, who first published a version of this commandment in 1968, often saw people with scrupulosity doubting the efficacy of their confession unless they'd prayed or fulfilled their penance perfectly. Father Miller tried to tell them perfection was not required—that their effort, complete or incomplete, was all that was required.

By stating clearly "for any reason," I've strengthened the original commandment by eliminating the excuses people might use to repeat penance(s).

The *Catechism of the Catholic Church* clearly teaches that "absolution takes away sin" (*CCC* 1459). Within the sacrament of reconciliation, it's the confession of sins and the absolution of the priest—not the perfect or imperfect act of the person who confesses—that completes the reception of the grace of the sacrament and takes away sin.

Penance is an act "performed by the penitent in order to repair the harm caused by sin and to re-establish habits befitting a disciple of Christ" (*CCC* 1494). It is distinct from the absolution of sin and the reception of the sacrament of reconciliation. Absolution is not dependent on the completion of penance, whether performed deliberately or accidentally, perfectly or imperfectly.

Let there be no confusion in this matter. The Church teaches that the only perfect remedy for sin—the only perfect satisfaction for sin—is found in Jesus Christ, "who alone expiated our sins once and for all" (*CCC* 1460). According to the Council of Trent (1551), as quoted in the *Catechism* (*CCC* 1460):

> The satisfaction that we make for our sins, however, is not so much ours as though it were not done through Jesus Christ. We who can do nothing ourselves, as if just by ourselves, can do all things with the cooperation of "him who strengthens" us (*DS* 1691, Philippians 4:13).

Even the most perfect act of penance performed with due diligence, without distraction, and with no stumbling upon words or concepts, would be imperfect. Only Jesus Christ, through his passion, death, and resurrection, is capable of the perfect act of satisfaction. We can participate in his saving action, but it's *his* saving action, not ours. It's not dependent on our thoughts or feelings; it's pure gift—sanctifying grace, manifested and received.

Fourth Commandment

You shall not be obsessively concerned about breaking your pre-Communion fast. Unless you put food and drink in your mouth and swallow it as a meal, you have not broken the fast.

Much of the anxiety about breaking the fast before Communion centers on extraneous matters. For example, lipstick and lip balm aren't food. Prescription medicines aren't food even if they're flavored. Snowflakes aren't food. You cannot break your fast unless you deliberately choose to eat in the same way you'd choose to eat a meal or a snack. No second thoughts are allowed regarding accidental swallowing of things that aren't considered food.

The fast is not a moral obligation; it's a devotional practice and discipline, intended to show additional respect for the sacrament of the Eucharist in the form of holy Communion. Here's what the *Code of Canon Law* says:

> 919. §1. A person who is to receive the Most Holy Eucharist is to abstain for at least one hour before holy communion from any food and drink, except for only water and medicine.
>
> §2. A priest who celebrates the Most Holy Eucharist two or three times on the same day can take something before the second or third celebration even if there is less than one hour between them.

> §3. The elderly, the infirm, and those who care for them can receive the Most Holy Eucharist even if they have eaten something within the preceding hour.

That the *Code* itself notes exceptions to the application of this devotional practice clearly identifies the practice as a discipline of the Church. It's most certainly not a practice that can't be dispensed with and that must be monitored with heroic effort.

Even in the most enthusiastically conservative interpretations of this law in all the journals I consulted, I was unable to discover any reference to sin or any canonical penalty. All authors agree that the pre-Communion fast is primarily a devotional practice.

Fifth Commandment

You shall not worry about powerful and vivid thoughts, desires, and imaginings involving sex and religion unless you deliberately generate them for the purpose of offending God.

All people have vivid thoughts and desires. The power of human imagination reflects our ability to dream and create. Since it's a gift from God, imagination gives glory and honor to God when we use this gift in service of our brothers and sisters.

This powerful gift is deeply dependent on our sensory perceptions. What we see, feel, hear, smell, and taste is part of what it means to be a living being. It's how God intended human life to be.

For example, when we smell the aroma of freshly baked bread, we might take a deep breath to enjoy the fullness of the smell. We deliberately smell the bread, and we fully intend to enjoy the smell—the action has our full consent and is totally expressive of our intent and purpose. But our other senses don't shut down—as we smell, we also taste, feel, and touch.

What might happen if, taking a cue from the warm overall feeling we get from the fresh bread, our senses also express the same feeling we experience in a romantic moment? Does this new feeling—which is perhaps highly sexual—mean we've chosen to deliberately sin against God? No. It's simply a feeling being expressed by one part of our senses in response to another part of our senses.

This interplay between thoughts, feelings, imagination, and all our creative and sensory responses is completely normal. This is the way God intends us to experience and enjoy life. People who don't experience life in this way have a severe physical and/or pathological illness.

Most of our experiences aren't as highly specialized and focused as this. Usually, we're not focusing on one sensory expression but are rather experiencing the full range of such expressions in all we experience. Occasionally, as in the bread example, we deliberately focus our sensory skills on one activity or experience. Other times our sensory gifts focus our attention on something that isn't deliberate or freely chosen but is nonetheless fully experienced and perhaps even enjoyed.

For example, we take a break in the afternoon from work and walk outside for a quick breath of fresh air. Out of the corner of our eye, we see a young woman who is vibrant, full of energy, and very appealing. She reminds us of ourselves when we were about her age or perhaps reminds us of our beloved spouse, and we find ourselves daydreaming of a time long in the past. That daydream may bring back an emotional experience that was part of our relationship, and we're now vividly and powerfully remembering and enjoying it.

Did we somehow provoke this memory that recalls the vivid

details of a long-ago moment? No, we chose to take a walk and get a breath of fresh air. But complementary moments can occur at any time and place. To avoid them, should we choose, out of an abundance of caution, to eliminate such experiences from our life? No. That is most certainly not God's will.

It is not the memory or the sensory perception that people with scrupulosity fear most. Often, they do not even fear sin. What people with scrupulosity fear more than anything else is not being fully in control. Their error, which is not deliberate or sinful, is in perceiving that people who don't have scrupulosity are always fully in control of their senses, their imaginations, and their responses. It is simply not true. We are not in control. We are, however, responsible for the choices we make. Each person ultimately determines if the action he or she chooses and consequently engages in brings him or her closer to his or her values or compromises them.

Sixth Commandment

You shall not worry about powerful and intense feelings, including sexual feelings or emotional outbursts, unless you deliberately generate them to offend God.

What is true concerning thoughts and desires can also be directly applicable to feelings. Often, a specific thought or desire is accompanied by a feeling. God gave us the ability to express our emotions, and doing so gives direct glory and honor to God.

On very rare occasions it may be appropriate to stifle a feeling or expression as inappropriate; however, it's usually healthy to permit feelings and emotions to be expressed. For example, it would be inappropriate to burst out laughing at an event in which silence is the expected and normal response. Such an outburst would be correctly identified as immature.

This commandment would be unnecessary if we were simply concerned about forming proper social skills. However, many people with scrupulosity choose to stifle, ignore, or downplay intense feelings and emotions for no reason other than an aversion to feeling as though they've lost control. Many people with scrupulosity believe that loss of a persistent sense of discipline somehow displeases the Lord and that it can never be appropriate to be intentionally expressive. Nothing could be further from the truth.

If a joke is funny, laugh hard. If you feel anger because you've been wronged, then anger is the correct response. If you feel sad and begin to cry, permit yourself a good cry. Laughing, crying, and being angry are normal human reactions. These experiences are not mortal, serious, or venial sins.

Seventh Commandment

You shall obey your confessor when he tells you never to repeat a general confession of sins already confessed to him or another confessor.

This commandment encompasses three issues: repeating general confession of sins to your confessor, repeating general confession of sins to other confessors, and following the spiritual counsel of your confessor in all matters of conscience.

A key component of scrupulosity is the seemingly never-ending impulse to repeat certain behaviors based on the misconceived notion that if a single act—in this case, a general confession—is performed perfectly, all doubt will be settled once and for all.

If it were that easy to heal scrupulosity, we would encourage everyone to seek this kind of perfection. But even if perfection were attainable, this practice still wouldn't be satisfactory, and it wouldn't free people with scrupulosity from fear and anxiety.

Repetition is not the solution. Repetition is a harmful manifestation of the obsessiveness and compulsiveness that accompany scrupulosity. Obsessive and compulsive repetition of a single action is unhealthy and counterproductive. Repetition is the disorder itself, cleverly masquerading as an antidote to doubt, fear, and anxiety. It's people with a scrupulous conscience in action.

Confessors forbid repetition of confessions not to deprive penitents of sacramental grace, but because confessors understand that repetition is harmful and counterproductive.

The entire scenario is made more complicated by the second component of this commandment: when penitents try to get around the rule by seeing additional confessors. It's at least less than honest to seek out another confessor to engage in this kind of repetitive behavior. It might even be a form of deceit.

Repeating confessions, whether to the same confessor or a variety, is harmful and not conducive either to spiritual growth or the healthy management of scrupulosity. Repetition isn't an act of piety or devotion; it's an act of desperation that leaves both the confessor and the penitent dissatisfied and unfulfilled. General confession isn't a sacramental remedy; it simply fuels obsession and compulsion. The doubt returns with even more energy and potential for continued injury.

Related to repetition of confession is the impulse to repeatedly examine your conscience for sin. For people with scrupulosity, the examination of conscience is counterproductive. When you use an examination to prepare for the sacrament, you—a scrupulous person—see yourself in each sin that is included in the examen. This is not the intent or the purpose of this spiritual tool/practice. Engaging in either the examen or the general confession is not recommended and should not be a component of your spiritual practice.

Leave all sins confessed and unconfessed in a sacramental confession in the hands of the Lord. Trust in his loving mercy and forgiveness.

A third component of this commandment is the directive to follow the spiritual counsel of your confessor in all matters of conscience. He is leading and guiding you with a patient and understanding heart. He's one of the avenues of God's good grace that's been given to you.

The consistent directive of the great saints throughout the ages and of all the priest-directors of Scrupulous Anonymous over the years has been to follow God's spiritual counsel in all things. When you choose a path that isn't supported by his strong and guiding hand, you take a step backward in your own spiritual growth and development.

It's most certainly not a sin to choose not to follow your confessor's directives, but it's counterproductive and not helpful.

Eighth Commandment

When you doubt your obligation to do or not do something, you will see your doubt as proof that there is no obligation.

This commandment is based on the moral principle that doubtful laws and obligations do not bind the conscience of people with scrupulosity. The great saint and our patron, St. Alphonsus Liguori, taught that this moral principle is the "habitual will of people with scrupulosity not to offend God." Saint Alphonsus was intimately familiar with the struggles of people with scrupulous conscience. He understood that men and women with scrupulosity desire above all else to please God. In the language of his century, this was called "habitual desire." Over the years, the priest-directors of Scrupulous Anonymous have been diligent in learning about the moral teaching of St. Alphonsus and applying his teachings as good and wise pastors. As saint, doctor of the Church, bishop, and moral theologian, he was (is) uniquely qualified to teach authoritatively on the formation of a moral conscience.

It's good to know that this very wise saint's teaching is so clear and straightforward. "There is no sin" are words we find most reassuring and words most people with scrupulosity are relieved to hear as often as necessary.

Ninth Commandment

When you are doubtful, you shall assume that the act of commission or omission you're in doubt about is not sinful.

The purpose of this commandment is to free a person with scrupulosity from the paralyzing fear and anxiety that are often part of the disorder. Saint Alphonsus teaches, "People with scrupulosity tend to fear that everything they do is sinful. The confessor should command them to act without restraint and to overcome their anxiety."

People in the grip of fear and anxiety caused by scrupulosity should deliberately act against the impulse that paralyzes them and instead choose a path that could lead to health and freedom.

Alphonsus continues, "The confessor may command people

with scrupulosity to conquer their anxiety and disregard it by freely doing whatever it tells them not to do. The confessor may assure the penitent that he or she need never confess such a thing."

Alphonsus says the paralyzing rigidity and anxiety are based on "groundless fear." The fear and anxiety are not guilt or remorse felt because of an action or inaction on the part of the penitent. Fear and anxiety are often painful symptoms of scrupulosity.

The inability to judge the difference between the reality of sin and the fear of sin is a common experience of the scrupulous disorder. Saint Alphonsus teaches that when this happens, both the confessor and the penitent should presume that the power of grace is at work in the life of God's people and not assume there is sin where no sin has occurred.

To sum it up: when making assumptions, assume grace, not sin.

Tenth Commandment

You shall put your total trust in Jesus Christ, knowing he loves you as only God can and that he will never allow you to lose your soul.

One of the most powerful experiences we can have is realizing that we're loved by the Lord exactly as we are—not as we might be one day. Freedom and confidence of faith come with this blessing.

This blessing is not reserved for a chosen few. It is intended for all of God's people in all times and places.

To me, this truth is liberating. I'm already the person I am, with all my strengths, talents, weaknesses, and liabilities. To know deep within my heart that God loves me exactly as I am gives me a framework for self-improvement and continued growth: I can grow when I'm invited to grow—not as a condition for love, but rather, as a consequence of that love. God, who invites me to grow daily in his grace, doesn't simply wait for me at the end of the journey as a reward for perseverance. He walks with me each step of the way.

For many people with scrupulosity, the experience of God's love is often tainted and skewed by their very poor perception of who they are before God. Scrupulosity distorts the fiber of grace that enables the gift of God's life and the gift of the Spirit, twisting them into an obstacle to God's grace and life.

APPENDIX D

Revisiting Ten Commandments for the Scrupulous Through the Lens of Inference-Based Cognitive Behavioral Therapy (I-CBT)

Frederick Aardema, PhD,
Constance Salhany, PhD, and
Rev. Thomas M. Santa, CSsR

Introduction

Continuing a Pastoral Legacy Through the Lens of I-CBT

Rev. Thomas M. Santa, CSsR's *Ten Commandments for the Scrupulous* has long served as a practical guide and source of relief for those suffering from scrupulosity. Building on Rev. Donald Miller, CSsR's 1968 version, Fr. Santa updated and refined these principles—in 1996 and again in 2013—for modern audiences, offering pastoral wisdom to help people navigate the relentless doubts that define this condition. This article revisits Fr. Santa's commandments through a contemporary psychological lens—specifically, inference-based cognitive behavioral therapy (I-CBT)—as a way of continuing his legacy of compassionate guidance.

Scrupulosity is not only a spiritual struggle but also a recognized form of obsessive-compulsive disorder (OCD), characterized by intrusive doubts about sin, morality, confession, personal worthiness, or spiritual failure. Historically, scrupulosity may be the earliest documented form of OCD, with descriptions dating back to early Christian and medieval writings. As discussed in the 2007 article "The Menace Within: Obsessions and the Self" by Dr. Frederick Aardema and Dr. Kieron O'Connor, early spiritual texts often describe individuals tormented by blasphemous or forbidden thoughts, accusing themselves of sins they had not committed—a phenomenon that closely parallels modern understandings of OCD. Jeremy Taylor's previously quoted seventeenth-century observation captures the essence of this experience: the tragic tendency to mistake innocence for guilt and virtues for flaws.

While obsessional doubts feel like moral warnings, I-CBT shows that they are rooted in reasoning and imaginative distortions—a confusion between imagination and reality—rather than in genuine spiritual failings. Fr. Santa's pastoral writings resonate with this perspective, as he consistently emphasizes clarity, trust, and the futility of endless self-accusation.

When the Ten Commandments for the Scrupulous were first written, their advice aligned with the predominant clinical treatments of the time, such as exposure and response prevention (ERP) and acceptance and commitment therapy (ACT). These approaches remain widely used and effective. In recent years, however, I-CBT has emerged as a novel, evidence-based treatment for OCD that shifts the focus from exposure and habituation to the reasoning errors at the heart of obsessional doubt.

I-CBT is rooted in the understanding that OCD is fundamentally a disorder of false and artificially created doubt, disconnected from present reality and sensory experience. As Dr. Frederick Aardema, co-founder of I-CBT, has described, obsessional doubt arises from inferential confusion—a process by which imagined, hypothetical possibilities are mistaken for real threats or moral failings.

While all evidence-based approaches seek to help individuals stop giving obsessive doubts undue importance, I-CBT offers a unique explanation for how these doubts come to feel relevant in the first place. A key contribution of I-CBT is its focus on how individuals with OCD mistake abstract, hypothetical possibilities for real probabilities, treating these imagined scenarios as if they were relevant moral doubts. Instead of engaging with the content of these doubts, I-CBT helps individuals step back from the obsessional narrative and reconnect with the evidence of their senses and their authentic experience.

Importantly, I-CBT is value-neutral. It does not attempt to challenge or alter religious beliefs or moral values, nor does it require exposure to unwanted thoughts or acceptance of anything contrary to one's values. Instead, it targets the process by which OCD hijacks reasoning, creating confusion between imagination and reality. This makes I-CBT highly compatible with faith traditions, as it helps individuals reconnect with the clarity of direct experience, restoring peace and trust while allowing them to step out of the false, imagined doubts that distort their practice of faith.

The aim of this article is to provide insights on Fr. Santa's commandments through the lens of I-CBT, highlighting the natural complementarity between his pastoral wisdom and I-CBT's focus on correcting reasoning and imaginative distortions. Many of Fr. Santa's observations—such as his emphasis on what is "clear and certain" and the pointlessness of repetitive confession—resonate strongly with I-CBT's approach to obsessive doubt.

Faith, at its heart, involves trust—even when complete certainty is absent. Scrupulosity, by contrast, demands answers to doubts that were never real to begin with. By integrating Fr. Santa's spiritual guidance with I-CBT's reasoning-based framework, we aim to help people distinguish between genuine moral reflection and OCD's false alarms, freeing them to live and practice their faith with confidence, compassion, and peace.

I-CBT and the Ten Commandments: A Shared Focus on Clarity and Trust

Fr. Santa's Ten Commandments for the Scrupulous offer practical, pastoral guidance for quieting the endless cycle of "what ifs" that plague those with scrupulosity. His commandments encourage trust, clarity, and an honest acceptance of what is real and certain instead of hypothetical fears or imagined sins. I-CBT shares this same foundation, although it approaches the issue from a psychological rather than theological standpoint.

I-CBT views scrupulosity as a problem of reasoning and imagination rather than a problem of belief. Obsessional doubt does not arise from genuine moral failings but from a reasoning error in which abstract, hypothetical possibilities are mistaken for real threats. For example, a person may begin to doubt whether he or she has offended God not because of any concrete action or evidence, but because the person's imagination constructs a "what if" scenario that feels compelling. This confusion is not about faith or values; it arises when an unjustified doubt replaces direct experience with imagined possibilities, giving these doubts a false sense of urgency and relevance.

In this way, I-CBT complements Fr. Santa's guidance. While the Ten Commandments for the Scrupulous invite individuals to let go of unnecessary guilt and encourage them to trust in God's mercy, I-CBT equips them with tools to help them recognize and break out of the obsessional narrative that fuels doubt. Both perspectives emphasize the importance of clarity—seeing what is actually present rather than what is imagined—and both encourage a return to trust, whether that trust is placed in divine grace, in one's own senses, or in the reality of the present moment.

First Commandment

You shall not confess sins you have already confessed.

Fr. Santa emphasizes that a confession made sincerely and clearly is valid the first time. For the scrupulous person, however, OCD generates obsessional doubt—a sense that the confession "didn't count" or "wasn't complete," which drives the urge to repeat it. In I-CBT terms, this urge is not a sign of unresolved sin but the result of reasoning and imaginative distortions in which the mind gives weight to imagined scenarios ("Maybe I left something out," or "What if I wasn't fully honest?") as if they were real evidence. This is often called *reverse reasoning*, where a feeling of doubt ("I don't feel forgiven") is mistakenly treated as proof that forgiveness did not occur.

I-CBT highlights that obsessional doubt is artificially created—it arises not from genuine moral discernment but from a reasoning and imaginative process disconnected from the senses and from reality. The sense of incompleteness or lingering anxiety after confession is not a moral warning but a symptom of OCD's obsessional narrative. Each repetition of confession attempts to resolve a problem that never truly existed.

Resisting the urge to re-confess is, therefore, an act of trust in what is real and complete rather than in the imagined imperfections that OCD presents. By not repeating confession, the individual steps out of the obsessional narrative and aligns with what he or she knows to be true: that the original confession was valid. I-CBT reframes this stance as choosing evidence from the here-and-now (the fact of having confessed) over "what if" thinking. As Fr. Santa writes, "When you refuse to engage the feeling of doubt...the wave of anxiety passes." Recognizing that the doubt is artificial, not a true moral signal, is a key step in breaking OCD's cycle of false reasoning.

Second Commandment

You shall confess only sins that are clear and certain.

Fr. Santa emphasizes that doubtful sins "don't count," and that confessing what is uncertain can be harmful rather than helpful. This wisdom aligns closely with I-CBT, which teaches that obsessional doubt is not evidence of wrongdoing, but the product of distorted reasoning and imagination. Again, obsessional doubt is *not* a moral signal; it does not reveal the presence of sin or moral failure. Instead, it reflects a breakdown in imagination and reasoning in which abstract and hypothetical scenarios are treated as if they were concrete realities.

From an I-CBT perspective, obsessional doubts are often abstract and disconnected from direct evidence. They rarely concern real-life uncertainty, which arises from situations that can be resolved by observation or action. Instead, they thrive on the *idea* of something being wrong: *Maybe I sinned but didn't notice it. What if I secretly intended to do wrong? Perhaps I'm just trying to convince myself I didn't sin.*

These doubts are rooted in imagination, not reality. They exist in a mental "what if" space, detached from the here-and-now. In I-CBT, this arises from dismissing direct experience—the evidence of the senses, the memory, and self-knowledge—and replacing it with abstract reasoning or moral hypotheticals.

Fr. Santa's call to confess only what is clear and certain aligns with the I-CBT principle of trusting what is real, direct, and observable rather than what is imagined. If a sin is not clear, it falls into the realm of abstract possibility, which does not require confession. Feelings of doubt, unease, or guilt are not evidence of wrongdoing; they are symptoms of OCD's obsessional narrative. As I-CBT puts it, feelings are not facts.

When scrupulous doubts arise, one can presume innocence and rely on the clarity of prior actions and intentions instead of chasing hypothetical wrongdoings. As Fr. Santa notes, doubt itself is part of being human, not proof of sinfulness. I-CBT expands on this by explaining that obsessional doubt is not even normal doubt—it is artificially created by the imagination and sustained by distrust of the senses and self. Recognizing this distortion allows the person to return to reality and anchor him- or herself in his or her true moral intent.

Third Commandment

You shall not repeat your penance or any of the words of your penance after confession—for any reason.

Fr. Santa, following Fr. Miller's earlier guidance, reminds us that penance does not need to be performed flawlessly or repeated for the sacrament to be effective. The grace of absolution does not depend on perfect concentration or exact words; it flows from the sacrament itself. Yet, for the scrupulous person, the mind often generates "what if" scenarios: *What if I didn't say it perfectly? What if I missed a word? What if it doesn't count?* This leads to compulsive repetition, which is essentially a form of mental checking.

In I-CBT, repetition is understood as an attempt to "fix" a problem that never actually existed. The doubt that drives repetition is imaginary, created by the obsession rather than by real evidence of error. An imaginary doubt cannot be resolved through repeated action; the repetition does nothing to address the root issue, because the problem exists only in the mind's imagined scenarios. The solution is to step back into reality and recognize that nothing was wrong in the first place.

I-CBT teaches that compulsive repetition arises from giving weight to "what if" possibilities rather than trusting what already has been completed. The focus shifts from participation in grace to achievement of a subjective "just right" feeling. Ironically, the more one repeats, the more the doubt grows, as the act of repetition signals to the brain that something is truly wrong.

To counter this, I-CBT reframes penance as an act of trust rather than of performance. Once the person has completed penance, it is complete—whether or not it felt perfect. By refusing to repeat penance, the individual practices "exiting the bubble"—stepping out of imagination and back into the reality of a sacrament that was already valid and sufficient.

Fourth Commandment

You shall not worry about breaking your pre-Communion fast unless you deliberately put food or drink in your mouth and swallow as a meal.

Fr. Santa reassures the scrupulous that breaking the pre-Communion fast is not something that occurs by accident or through trivial actions, like swallowing saliva or using lip balm. The fast is an intentional, devotional practice, and it is only broken through deliberate acts of eating or drinking. For the scrupulous person, however, the mind often invents "what if" scenarios: *What if I swallowed something accidentally? What if I broke the fast without realizing it? What if God sees my carelessness as a sin?* These doubts arise not from real evidence, but from abstract reasoning disconnected from reality.

From an I-CBT perspective, these doubts are classic examples of obsessional reasoning—they start with the imagined possibility of wrongdoing and treat that possibility as if it really happened. OCD's obsessional narrative dismisses the evidence of the senses (e.g., *I didn't eat or drink anything*) and replaces it with hypothetical fears (*What if I somehow did but didn't notice?*). The person becomes stuck in his or her imagination, treating every small sensation or vague memory as potential proof of failure.

I-CBT emphasizes that real uncertainty can be resolved by looking to the present reality and direct evidence. For example, in reality, a person easily knows whether he or she has eaten or drunk something deliberately. Obsessional doubt, by contrast, never deals with real uncertainty—it manufactures an imaginary problem and then demands an impossible level of proof to resolve it. Trying to answer the "what if" questions that arise only strengthens the doubt, because the doubt was never based in reality to begin with.

The key, as both Fr. Santa and I-CBT suggest, is to trust one's intentions and the direct evidence of the moment. If the person did not take deliberate action to eat or drink, then the fast is intact. On the other hand, attempting to mentally "check" or review every detail of the past hour is like trying to solve an imaginary puzzle—it only keeps the person stuck inside the obsessional narrative. The path to peace lies in the person's returning to reality, recognizing that the doubt was artificially created, and trusting both his or her lived experience and sincere intent.

Fifth Commandment

You shall not worry about powerful and vivid thoughts, desires, and imaginings involving sex and religion unless you deliberately generate them for the purpose of offending God.

Fr. Santa reminds us that vivid or powerful thoughts—especially those involving sex or religion—are not sinful unless they are deliberately generated with the intention of offending God. Yet for the scrupulous person, the sudden appearance of such thoughts can feel deeply disturbing, as if their mere presence is proof of wrongdoing. This is precisely where I-CBT provides a critical insight: these thoughts are not signals of hidden intent or moral failure—they are phantom thoughts, mental constructs born from the obsessional doubt itself.

In I-CBT, what many call "intrusive thoughts" are not random or autonomous. They are imagined constructs created by the obsessional narrative. Once OCD plants the seed of doubt—*What if I'm blasphemous?*—the mind becomes hyper-focused, scanning for evidence of danger or hidden intent. This checking and monitoring create vivid mental images or sensations, which are mistaken as proof of sin. OCD flips the cause and effect: doubt creates the thought, but it feels like the thought came first, validating the fear. This reasoning error is called *reversing causal direction*.

Fr. Santa's guidance on not worrying about these thoughts or imaginings aligns perfectly with I-CBT's principle of recognizing these experiences as products of imagination, not of reality. They do not reflect your true self, intentions, or values. They are the echoes of OCD's story, not evidence of sin. Trying to suppress or analyze them only strengthens the illusion, while acknowledging their false origin weakens their power.

The key is to step back and recognize the trick at play. These thoughts and sensations are constructed by the mind's immersion in doubt, not sin. Just as a person with contamination OCD experiences phantom sensations of feeling sticky or dirty, the scrupulous person experiences mental images or feelings of moral failure that are illusions. I-CBT invites the person to exit the narrative and return to the reality of his or her true moral intent, which remains unblemished.

Sixth Commandment

You shall not worry about powerful and intense feelings, including sexual feelings or emotional outbursts, unless you deliberately generate them to offend God.

Fr. Santa reminds us that feelings—whether joy, anger, sadness, or even strong sexual emotions—are not sinful in themselves. They are part of the natural range of the human experience and, when expressed appropriately, give glory to God. Many scrupulous individuals, however, fear that the mere presence of strong feelings is evidence of moral failure or spiritual weakness. They may try to suppress, control, or neutralize these feelings out of fear that losing emotional control somehow displeases God.

In I-CBT, this suppression of natural feelings is understood as a disconnection from the experience of direct, unfiltered perception of reality as it is. Before doubt arises, feelings are simply felt experiences, neither good nor bad. It is only when OCD introduces obsessional doubt—*"What if my anger is sinful?"* or *"What if this feeling means I am corrupt?"*—that emotions are misinterpreted as dangerous or morally suspect. I-CBT teaches that obsessional doubt is not a moral indicator, but a combination of reasoning and imaginative distortions that replace reality with "what if" scenarios.

Just as Fr. Santa encourages us to laugh freely at a joke or cry when we feel sad, I-CBT emphasizes reconnecting with the original experience of the moment without overanalyzing it. Feelings are transient, not verdicts on character. Anger, joy, or arousal arise naturally from life's situations, but OCD magnifies them, asking for impossible certainty: *What if this feeling means I want something bad?* In reality, feelings are simply signals of being alive—what matters is intention and deliberate choice, not the presence of emotion itself.

By allowing emotions to flow without judgment, the individual moves out of the obsessional narrative and returns to the here-and-now. Both Fr. Santa's pastoral advice and I-CBT agree that the key to peace is trusting direct experience rather than mistrusting it through the lens of OCD.

Seventh Commandment

You shall obey your confessor when he tells you never to repeat a general confession of sins already confessed to him or another confessor.

Fr. Santa highlights how the scrupulous person often feels compelled to repeat general confessions, as though doing it "one more time" might finally resolve an imagined incompleteness. But, as he wisely points out, repetition is not a remedy—it is the problem itself. The doubt that drives the repetition is not a true moral issue, but an illusion created by scrupulosity.

In I-CBT, this compulsion is understood as the result of false doubt, not simply due to any rigid need for certainty. The individual acts and feels as if something is unresolved when, in fact, nothing needs fixing—the confession was already complete and valid. The obsessive urge to "go back and check" or confess again is like trying to fix a typo on a blank page: there is nothing there to fix. I-CBT shows that repeating confession is a way of engaging with the obsessional narrative—feeding an imaginary problem instead of recognizing that the doubt itself is baseless.

Obeying the confessor's instruction to stop repeating confessions is therefore a way of returning to reality. It means trusting what is already known and what has already been experienced—*I confessed, I received absolution, it is done*—rather than being pulled into endless "what if" scenarios. I-CBT frames this as refusing to reason from imagination and instead relying on direct evidence (the memory of the confession and the sacrament itself).

Fr. Santa also warns against trying to sidestep this commandment by seeking other confessors. I-CBT describes this as compulsive reassurance-seeking driven by a false belief that resolution lies in more confession, when the real solution is to recognize that there was never a real problem in the first place. Trusting the confessor's guidance is not about perfection—it is about refusing to participate in OCD's cycle of invented doubts.

Eighth Commandment

When you doubt your obligation to do or not do something, you will see your doubt as proof that there is no obligation.

Fr. Santa draws on the teaching of St. Alphonsus Liguori, who recognized that the scrupulous person's habitual will is to avoid offending God. When a doubt arises about an obligation, this very doubt reveals that there is no obligation—because if there were a clear duty, the person would already act without question. This principle is deeply reassuring for those trapped by scrupulosity, where doubt is mistaken for moral responsibility.

From an I-CBT perspective, this aligns with the understanding that OCD hijacks a person's values and sense of responsibility, turning them inward as a weapon. The person's genuine desire to be good and faithful becomes misapplied to abstract, imagined scenarios: *What if I failed to honor this holy day without realizing it?* or *Maybe I had an obligation I didn't know about, and I've already sinned.*

These doubts are not rooted in real-world obligations; instead, they stem from reasoning distortions and imaginative distortions in which the mind invents hypothetical obligations detached from evidence. OCD thrives on this by conflating moral values with the endless pursuit of imaginary "what ifs."

I-CBT teaches that moral reasoning must be grounded in original experience—in what is directly known and observable—not in hypothetical constructs. If you cannot clearly identify the obligation in the present moment, the doubt itself is proof that the "obligation" is part of OCD's narrative, not of reality. In this sense, I-CBT helps the individual reclaim his or her values, reminding the person that faithfulness does not mean endlessly scanning for moral traps, but living according to what is real, here, and now.

By seeing doubt for what it is—a misapplication of values rather than a true moral warning—the person can step out of the cycle of fear and return to authentic trust. This is fully in line with Fr. Santa's teaching: when the doubt itself is the only "evidence" of wrongdoing, there is no obligation.

Ninth Commandment

When you are doubtful, you shall assume that the act of commission or omission about which you're in doubt is not sinful, and you shall proceed without dread of sin.

Fr. Santa advises that when doubt arises about whether something was sinful, the safest and healthiest approach is to proceed as though no sin has occurred. For the scrupulous person, this may feel counterintuitive because the doubt itself feels morally urgent. Yet, as Fr. Santa notes, these doubts are not a sign of moral failure—they are part of the scrupulous condition itself, driven by fear rather than reality.

According to I-CBT, the key is recognizing that everything stems from the initial obsessional doubt. OCD creates a false question—*What if I sinned?* or *What if I failed to do something I should have done?*—even when there is no real event or evidence to support it. In omission doubts especially, OCD treats the absence of clear memory or evidence as proof that something must have gone wrong. I-CBT teaches the inverse of this reasoning: the absence of evidence means there is no reason to engage the doubt, not that the doubt is valid.

Once the person can see the initial doubt for what it is—a mental fabrication rather than a real moral issue—the rest of the cycle begins to collapse on its own. Anxiety, dread, and compulsions are all fueled by this false starting point. This is why both Fr. Santa and I-CBT encourage the individual to move forward without engaging the doubt. There is nothing to resolve because nothing is wrong. When the person stops trying to answer the doubt, the accompanying fear and compulsions lose their power. Instead of endlessly analyzing intentions or replaying events, one must simply acknowledge, *This is just OCD talking; it's not reality.*

In this sense, obeying this commandment is not denial, but clarity. It is choosing to treat false alarms as what they are—false—and trusting that genuine moral concerns do not arrive in the form of relentless "what if" scenarios.

Tenth Commandment

You shall put your total trust in Jesus Christ, knowing that he loves you as only God can and that he will never allow you to lose your soul.

Fr. Santa reminds us that the heart of faith is trust—trust that God's love is constant, unconditional, and not dependent on our feelings or performance. Many people with scrupulosity struggle to believe this because OCD distorts their perception of grace, turning God's love into a source of fear and self-accusation for them. As Fr. Santa writes, "God loves me exactly as I am.... He walks with me each step of the way." This is the truth that OCD tries to obscure.

Through the lens of I-CBT, obsessional doubt generates false alarms about salvation. The mind imagines scenarios, such as *What if God rejects me?* or *What if I didn't do enough to be saved?* and treats these hypothetical fears as though they were real. This reflects what I-CBT calls a confusion between imagined possibilities and reality. The presence of doubt is not a sign that grace is absent; it is simply the result of distorted reasoning and imagination.

I-CBT helps individuals recognize that no amount of mental checking, repeated prayer, or endless reassurance can create salvation or prove God's love. These compulsive attempts only strengthen the illusion that something is wrong. Salvation is not attained through mental effort but received through grace and entrusted to Divine Mercy. By stepping out of the obsessional narrative, a person can return to the lived reality of faith: a relationship grounded in trust rather than fear.

To follow this commandment from an I-CBT perspective is to see the doubt for what it is—an illusion—and to rest in the truth of God's presence and love, even when OCD tries to claim otherwise.

Conclusion: I-CBT and the Path Beyond Scrupulosity

Fr. Santa's Ten Commandments for the Scrupulous offer timeless pastoral wisdom: trust, clarity, and freedom from the endless loops of fear. Viewed through the lens of I-CBT, these principles gain an additional psychological dimension—one that focuses not on theology or morality, but on the distorted reasoning and imagination that drive obsessive doubt.

I-CBT is not about accepting uncertainty, challenging values, or changing beliefs. In fact, people with scrupulous obsessions are often deeply committed to their values, sometimes to the point of being misled by their own sincerity. The real issue is not rigidity, but doubt—false, artificially created doubt that masquerades as moral concern. I-CBT helps individuals recognize that these doubts are not spiritual warnings, but mental fabrications created by a reasoning process that confuses imagined "what if" scenarios with reality.

When the illusion of doubt is seen for what it is, the entire chain of anxiety, dread, and compulsions begins to unravel. Both Fr. Santa's guidance and I-CBT point toward the same freedom:

the ability to live in alignment with one's faith and values without being hijacked by obsessive questioning.

For those seeking additional support, the following suggestions may help:

- Therapy: Find a faith-respecting ICBT therapist at www.icbt.online, which offers resources and a directory of therapists that offer ICBT.
- Self-help: Resolving OCD, a two-volume series written by Dr. Frederick Aardema, provides a detailed, step-by-step framework for dismantling obsessive doubt through the ICBT approach.
- Spiritual support: Pair ICBT with trusted spiritual direction to ensure that your faith and mental-health efforts complement each other.
- Pastoral community: The website www.scrupulousanonymous.org offers a wealth of resources, including the free monthly *Scrupulous Anonymous* newsletter, decades of Q&A, and articles offering spiritual encouragement to complement both ICBT and pastoral guidance.

In the end, both Fr. Santa and I-CBT emphasize the same truth: faith is not found in compulsive checking or in answering every doubt, but in the clarity that comes from trusting what is real. By combining pastoral wisdom with a reasoning-based therapeutic approach, individuals can move beyond OCD's false alarms and step into a life of confidence, peace, and authentic spiritual connection.

Additional Resources

Books

A Guide for the Scrupulous: Spiritual Practices, Critical Beliefs, Helpful Prayers, Rev. Thomas M. Santa, CSsR (Liguori Publications, 2025).

Resolving OCD (Volume 1): Understanding Your Obsessional Experience, Frederick Aardema, PhD (Mount Royal Publishing, 2024).

Resolving OCD (Volume 2): Advanced Strategies for Overcoming Obsessional Doubt, Frederick Aardema, PhD (Mount Royal Publishing, 2024).

Understanding Scrupulosity, 4th ed., Rev. Thomas M. Santa, CSsR (Liguori Publications, 2025).

Websites

I-CBT Online, icbt.online. Information on the history and practice of I-CBT, resources, a therapist directory, and more information on the *Resolving OCD* series.

Managing Scrupulosity, managingscrupulosity.com. Resources and support for the scrupulous and for priests/confessors from Rev. Thomas M. Santa, CSsR.

Scrupulous Anonymous, scrupulousanonymous.org. A monthly newsletter, articles, reflections, Q&A, and helpful resources from the Redemptorists.

Bibliography

Aardema, Frederick, PhD and Kieran O'Connor, PhD. "The Menace Within: Obsessions and the Self." *Journal of Cognitive Psychotherapy,* September 1, 2007.

Santa, Fr. Thomas M., CSsR. "Ten Commandments for the Scrupulous (2013)." Scrupulous Anonymous. *https://scrupulousanonymous.org/wp-content/uploads/2015/10/Ten_Commandments_for_the_Scrupulous_2013.pdf*

Taylor, Jeremy. *The Rule of Conscience (Ductor dubitantium).* London: Richard Royston, 1660.

Three Hundred Years of Psychiatry, 1535–1860, edited by Richard Hunter and Ida Macalpine. Oxford, England: Oxford University Press, 1963.

Acknowledgments

I wish to thank all the scrupulous people I have encountered over the years. You were so patient with me when I did not yet understand. You were so honest with me, even when it was painful. You opened a place in your hearts for me despite the risk of being hurt even more. Despite the suffering you endured, you never wavered in your hope that you might be freed from or at least find a way to manage the disorder. You know and understand that scrupulosity is never suffered alone. Those who love and care for you and those who minister to you, even if they do not understand what you are talking about, are people for whom you are thankful.

Rev. Paul Coury, CSsR, has joined me in this important ministry and has been a real lifesaver for many people. I wish to thank those priests and bishops who suffer with the disorder and who have encouraged me, as well as the therapists who want to learn about the Catholic perspective of healing so they can best serve their clients. Thank you to Dr. Larry Jehling, who funded the original www.managingscrupulosity.com and who encouraged me to teach others who had been called to ministry with the scrupulous. And of course I want to thank those who, through their honesty and vulnerability, have enabled not only their own healing but also the healing of others with the disorder.

I remember, in gratitude, Jay and John. For them, scrupulosity became overwhelming and claimed their lives. Thankfully, I know they are safely in the arms of their Redeemer and suffer no more. I know there are others who have suffered the same fate; I pray for them daily, and I am thankful for the gift of who they were.

Rev. Thomas M. Santa, CSsR

About the Author

Rev. Thomas M. Santa, CSsR, is the president and publisher of Liguori Publications, his second assignment as the company's leader. Professed as a Redemptorist in 1973, his ministries have included directing Scrupulous Anonymous and Managing Scrupulosity, writing reflections for the *Scrupulous Anonymous* newsletter, and retreat work.

NOTES

NOTES

NOTES

NOTES

NOTES

CATHOLIC. PASTORAL. TRUSTED.

ISBN 978-0-764-82911-6